Contents

Coronary heart disease:
Are women special?

EDITED BY
IMOGEN SHARP

National Forum for Coronary Heart Disease Prevention
Hamilton House, Mabledon Place, London WC1H 9TX

Acknowledgements

The National Forum for Coronary Heart Disease Prevention would like to thank all those who helped in the production of this report. Particular thanks are due to:

- **The Steering Group:**
Maggie Sanderson, British Dietetic Association (Chair)
Imogen Sharp, Director, National Forum for Coronary Heart Disease Prevention
Professor John Goodwin, Chairman (1987-1993), National Forum for Coronary Heart
    Disease Prevention
Dr Bobbie Jacobson, Director of Public Health, East London and The City Health Authority
Professor Desmond Julian, Chairman, National Forum for Coronary Heart Disease
    Prevention (formerly Consultant Medical Director, British Heart Foundation)
Jeanette Longfield, formerly Senior Policy Analyst, Coronary Prevention Group
Professor Michael Oliver, Emeritus Professor, National Heart and Lung Institute
Heather Waring, Education Manager, British Heart Foundation

- **The Expert Meeting Chairs:**
Dame Rosemary Rue, Past President, British Medical Association and Faculty of Public
    Health Medicine
Shirley Goodwin, Visiting Fellow, King's Fund Institute

- All the speakers whose papers form the basis of this report

- The participants at the expert meeting from which this report derives

- The British Heart Foundation for providing funding for the expert meeting and this
    report

- The President and Treasurer of the Royal College of Physicians for providing the
    meeting facilities

- Rosie Leyden who helped with editing, and Mary Sayers who helped to update the
    data. Thanks also to Mike Rayner and Lesley Rogers for their contributions.

ISBN 1 874279 03 9

National Forum for Coronary Heart Disease Prevention
Hamilton House, Mabledon Place, London WC1H 9TX

Registered Company Number: 2487644 Registered Charity Number: 803286

VAT Number: 564 6088 18

Report produced by Wordworks (London W4 2HY). Design by Sue Dransfield.

Foreword

Coronary heart disease: Are women special? is an initiative of the National Forum for Coronary Heart Disease Prevention, comprising an expert meeting and this report. It arose from concerns that coronary heart disease (CHD) is often viewed as a disease that afflicts only men, and that women may have different needs in terms of its prevention and treatment. Health education materials, the media and the medical press may perpetuate this image of CHD as a man's disease among both the public and health professionals by using images of mostly male victims. Although the differences between women and men have been discussed sporadically several times over the past 20 years, the issues have not been addressed in policy terms.

Almost all the Forum member organisations participated in the expert meeting from which this report derives. The recommendations given in Chapter 3 therefore represent the broad consensus view of the Forum.

We hope that the report will highlight women's needs in CHD, and that the issues and recommendations will be taken up by organisations and individuals whose work impinges on CHD prevention. Research, policy development, education and service provision all fall under the auspices of one or more of the Forum member organisations, so there is great potential to address this previously neglected area. We are pleased that discussion continues and that the profile of many of the issues has increased since the Forum's expert meeting. Whenever CHD is being considered, the question should be asked: 'Are women special?'

The health strategies for England, Scotland, Wales and Northern Ireland provide the opportunity to place these issues properly on the national agenda.

An editorial in the *New England Journal of Medicine* on the topic of women and heart disease concluded that:

> *"the problem is to convince both the lay and medical sectors that CHD is also a woman's disease, not a man's disease in disguise. Neither women nor their physicians fully recognise that myocardial infarction is the leading cause of death among women in the United States"*.[1]

The issues are also true for the UK, and we hope that this report will convince its readers that CHD is an important problem for women too.

We are grateful for the advice of representatives of several Forum member organisations: the British Dietetic Association, the British Heart Foundation, the Coronary Prevention Group, and the Royal College of Physicians of Edinburgh.

We would particularly like to thank the British Heart Foundation for making the expert meeting and this report possible, by generously providing funding.

Professor John Goodwin MD, FRCP, FACP(Hon), FACC
Chairman, National Forum for Coronary Heart Disease Prevention (1987-1993)

Ms Imogen Sharp MSc (Econ), Hon MFPHM
Director, National Forum for Coronary Heart Disease Prevention

---

Reference

1   Healy B. 1991. The Yentl Syndrome. *New England Journal of Medicine*; 325: 274-276.

CHAPTER 1

Introduction

Coronary heart disease is the single leading cause of death among women. It kills some 76,000 women in the UK every year, and causes illness and disability for many more. It is also the largest single cause of premature death in women, accounting for almost 6,000 deaths each year in women under 65.

Despite this, coronary heart disease (CHD) is often viewed as a male disease. Much of the research and discussion on the causes, prevention, diagnosis and treatment of CHD so far has focused on men. The results of research among men may not apply to women, however, and this has implications for policy decisions on both prevention and treatment of CHD among women.

The purpose of this report is to improve understanding of CHD risk in women, and to stimulate action to address this risk. Both science and policy issues are addressed. The report reviews evidence on CHD risk in women, outlines the importance and patterns of the risk factors, and discusses the policy implications for national and local agencies, and for women themselves. It has been developed from an expert meeting held by the National Forum for Coronary Heart Disease Prevention. Health professionals, policy makers, scientific researchers and consumer groups all participated in the discussion. Since the Forum's expert meeting in 1991, the issue of CHD in women has gained greater attention, both nationally and internationally. More research has emerged, including the results of several much needed UK studies, and this information has also been incorporated.

The report asks: Are women special? The answer must be 'No', and 'Yes'.

International comparisons show a league table ranking for CHD that is similar for women and men: rates among women in the UK, as among men, are near the top. Differences in CHD rates between countries outweigh the sex differences within a country. The same environmental factors seem to be operating in both women and men, so broad public health strategies to reduce CHD risk are likely to be similarly effective for both. Such strategies will also reduce the risk of other diseases.

But within each country, there are sex differences in CHD rates, in risk factors, and in presentation, which deserve special attention and special strategies. Rates of CHD in the UK have not been falling as fast in women as in men.

Women have lower rates of CHD than men at any age: although women's rates increase with age, they never catch up with men's. The proportion eventually dying of CHD is similar in both sexes, but the disease occurs up to 10 years later in women. There are several possible explanations, both biological and behavioural, as the individual chapters outline.

Firstly, women in the UK have a lower prevalence of many of the risk factors for CHD. They have traditionally smoked less and, at younger ages, they have lower blood pressure and blood cholesterol levels. Women also have a more favourable lipid profile: their higher HDL cholesterol levels and lower triglyceride levels may partly explain the sex differences in risk. Some of women's advantage may now be changing, however: the sex difference in smoking rates among adults has virtually disappeared, for example, and girls are more likely to smoke than boys. Will CHD rates begin to increase among women, as lung cancer has?

Secondly, women seem to tolerate risk factors better than men. The relative risk of CHD associated with a high level of a risk factor compared to a low level is the same for women as for men, and 'dose-responses' exist. However, for any given level of the risk factor, the absolute risk of CHD is much lower among women than men. Thus, in women, a given risk factor is associated with a lower CHD risk. Women are less physically active than men and more likely to be obese. Their diet is higher in saturated fat (as a percentage of energy) than that of men. Even after the menopause, women seem to tolerate CHD risk factors better than men of the same age: they have higher blood pressure levels, for example, but lower CHD risk.

Thirdly, hormonal differences may account for some of the sex differences: women's higher oestrogen levels seem to offer some protection against CHD. The changes associated with the menopause have an adverse effect on some of the risk factors, such as blood lipid levels, and add to the risk of CHD. But post-menopausal women still have a lower risk of CHD than similarly aged men. Furthermore, national mortality statistics indicate that the reduced sex ratio in CHD rates in older groups is due to a relative slowing down in the increase in men's rates after about age 50, rather than an acceleration in women's rates of CHD.

Finally, there are sex differences in the clinical presentation of CHD, and in the natural history of the disease. Angina – the most common form of presentation of CHD in women – is as prevalent in women as men; heart attack rates are lower; but silent heart attacks are common. Women with CHD also have a worse prognosis than men, and are more likely to die from the disease, partly due to their older age and greater prevalence of complicating factors such as hypertension and diabetes. It may also be partly due to the effect of the male image of CHD on women's perceptions and on the judgements of health professionals. Studies consistently show a sex difference in patient care for CHD: even when symptoms are identical, women are less likely to be referred for diagnosis and treatment.

While the differences in CHD between women and men have no special implications for broad public health measures to reduce the risk, they do have implications for targeted interventions and for clinical decisions on prevention and treatment. The existence of sex differences means a need for some special approaches to CHD in women.

This report tackles many of the issues, but also raises many questions. It highlights the obvious neglect of women in research and policy on CHD – on risk factors, health-related behaviour, preventive interventions, diagnosis, treatment and rehabilitation. There are few randomised trials to evaluate preventive and therapeutic measures in women, and to answer questions specific to women.

Many of the special issues for women remain unanswered, and in particular why women in manual social classes, South Asian women, and women with diabetes have such high rates of CHD. How important are HDL cholesterol and triglycerides; obesity and the waist:hip ratio; the iron stores in the body; and social support? By neglecting women, the research community has not learnt as much about CHD as it could. Women *are* special and, in CHD as in other areas, men might gain from an understanding of them.

Overall, there is little research from which to derive policy for women. Policies are based largely on research among white, middle-aged men, but are the results equally appropriate for women? Without research in women, many interventions may be inappropriately implemented. The use of fixed cut-points for intervention on cholesterol and blood pressure is one example; the preventive use of HRT could be another.

The UK population is getting older, and CHD among women will become an increasingly important public health problem, as women live longer than men. The public, health professionals and policy makers need to recognise that CHD is the leading single cause of death among women, and a major cause of illness and disability. The national health strategies all feature CHD as a key area for action, and provide a valuable vehicle for addressing many of the concerns. Prevention needs to start in the young.

In the United States – where CHD among women has been called the 'silent epidemic' – the Women's Health Initiative has been set up by the National Institutes of Health to address the inequalities for women in health research and care, for major causes of death and disability. The 10-year, $500 million initiative, begun in 1991, includes clinical trials and observational studies, and interventions to promote healthy behaviour among women.

Does CHD in women in the UK deserve a similar priority? This report shows that it does.

CHAPTER 2

The National Forum for Coronary Heart Disease Prevention

The National Forum for Coronary Heart Disease Prevention was established in 1983, initially as the National Coordinating Committee for Coronary Heart Disease Prevention, following the Canterbury conference *Action to prevent coronary heart disease.*

Within its aim to contribute to a reduction in coronary heart disease morbidity and mortality in the UK, the Forum has four central objectives:

● to keep under review the activities of member organisations in the field of coronary heart disease prevention and disseminate findings
● to identify areas of consensus, issues of controversy, and needs for action in the field of coronary heart disease prevention
● to facilitate the coordination of activities between interested organisations in the field of coronary heart disease prevention
● to make recommendations where appropriate.

The Forum currently coordinates the work of expert representatives from over 35 national organisations involved in coronary heart disease prevention in the UK, including the health services, professional bodies and voluntary organisations. Members also include several individual experts.

Member organisations of the National Forum for Coronary Heart Disease Prevention

Action on Smoking and Health (ASH)
Anticipatory Care Teams (ACT)
Association of Primary Care Facilitators
British Association for Cardiac Rehabilitation
British Cardiac Society
British Dietetic Association
British Heart Foundation
British Medical Association

British Nutrition Foundation
British Paediatric Association
Consumers' Association
CORDA
Coronary Prevention Group
Faculty of Public Health Medicine
Family Heart Association
Health Education Authority
Health Education Board for Scotland
Health Promotion Agency for Northern Ireland
Health Promotion Authority for Wales
Health Visitors' Association
Institution of Environmental Health Officers
National Association of Governors and Managers
National Association of Health Authorities and Trusts
Northern Ireland Chest, Heart and Stroke Association
Royal College of General Practitioners
Royal College of Nursing
Royal College of Physicians of Edinburgh
Royal College of Physicians of London
Royal College of Surgeons
Royal Institute of Public Health and Hygiene
Royal Pharmaceutical Society of Great Britain
Society of Cardiothoracic Surgeons
Society of Health Education and Health Promotion Specialists
Society of Occupational Medicine
Sports Council
Trades Union Congress

Observers
Department of Health
Department of Health and Social Services, Northern Ireland
Medical Research Council
Ministry of Agriculture, Fisheries and Food
National Consumer Council
Scottish Consumer Council
The Scottish Office, Home and Health Department
Welsh Office

In addition, a number of distinguished experts in the field have individual membership.

CHAPTER 3

The way forward.
Recommendations

Coronary heart disease has traditionally been perceived as a man's disease. Yet it is also the leading single cause of death among women in the UK, both above and below the age of 65. Each year, about 76,000 women in the UK die from coronary heart disease (CHD), which accounts for 23%, or one in four, of all deaths among women.

Death rates for CHD among women in the UK are among the highest in the world. Although women have lower CHD rates than men, women in Scotland and Northern Ireland have higher rates than men in countries with low rates such as France, Spain and Japan. Death rates from CHD in the UK are falling, but the declines are slower among women than men.

The international league table rankings for CHD among women and men are similar. The environmental determinants of CHD seem to affect women and men similarly, and preventive action targeted towards the general population is likely to be effective for both.

Within the UK, there are regional differences in CHD rates, social class differences, and ethnic variations among women, all of which need to be addressed. Women in regions with high CHD rates have higher rates than men in regions with low rates. The inverse social class gradient in CHD mortality rates is greater among women than among men, and appears to be widening, as in men.

South Asian women have particularly high rates of CHD: about 50% greater than other women living in England and Wales. The excess is greater among women than men. Afro-Caribbean women have low rates of CHD compared to the general population, but are less well protected than Afro-Caribbean men.

Diabetic women are also at particularly high risk: they have the same risk of CHD as all men. Diabetes imposes a greater risk of CHD among women than among men.

CHD is also an important cause of illness and disability among women. There are sex differences in the spectrum of clinical presentation, which need to be taken into account. Angina is as common in women as in men, and affects an estimated 900,000 women in the UK. Angina is the most common form of presentation among women with CHD. While heart attacks are less common among women, painless heart attacks are common, particularly in older ages. The male image of CHD may affect the diagnosis and treatment of CHD among women.

Although women live five or six years longer than men on average, their extra years of life are often years of disability, and CHD, stroke and cancer are major contributors. These conditions are highly preventable. The potential rise in CHD rates among women, with an increasingly ageing population, and as smoking among women begins to show its toll, is likely to have major consequences for the health service.

There is considerable scope for reducing the risk of CHD among women. The major risk factors – smoking, high blood cholesterol levels, and hypertension – are the same for women as for men, although they operate at a different level. Among older ages, the prevalence of classic risk factors is higher among women than among men. However, women may tolerate risks better than men: for any given level of risk factor, women have a smaller risk of CHD than men.

The potential for the prevention of CHD is greater than for breast cancer or cervical cancer in real terms, although many of the prevention strategies for CHD will also have an impact on other diseases, such as cancer. Action needs to be taken to prevent CHD before signs and symptoms of the disease appear.

The underlying challenges, in population terms, are similar for all CHD risk factors. They include social policy measures which take account of the large inverse social class gradient in CHD risk and the additional responsibilities of women in society, and which support health education measures. Poorer women should be the primary focus of any prevention strategies. While the differences between women and men in terms of CHD have no special implications for a population approach, they do for a high risk approach and clinical decision-making. Special strategies are also needed to target those most at risk.

Recommendations

This chapter sets out the Forum's major recommendations, arising from the expert meeting, to address the high rates of CHD among women in the UK. Chapters 4-10 give further policy options to address the risk factors, and a wider range of proposals for action is given in Chapter 11.

The recommendations highlight women's special needs in CHD, but most population prevention issues affect both women and men, and indeed will also help reduce the risks of other diseases. The focus should be on a long-term population approach, rather than the mass medication of a large number of women before the evidence is complete.

The Health of the Nation, and the parallel health strategies for Scotland, Wales and Northern Ireland, include targets for coronary heart disease and stroke. These could provide a valuable focus for implementing the recommendations, and tackling CHD among women.

EDUCATION AND AWARENESS

Public and professional education about women's risk of CHD is essential.

1   Women should be made aware of their risk of coronary heart disease, in order to respond to preventive health advice, and to recognise symptoms.

Health education materials, advertising, and articles on CHD directed towards the general public should feature women, in order to redress the balance of male stereotypes of heart disease victims.

•   A national education programme, to improve women's awareness of their risk of CHD, should be undertaken by health education agencies (including heart charities), health professionals, and the media.

2   Health professionals should be made aware of the risks of coronary heart disease among women.

Health care providers need to improve diagnosis, referral and treatment of women with symptoms of CHD, and to understand the possibilities for prevention or modification of risk factors among women. This applies to health professionals and health service managers in both primary care and hospital sectors including, for example, GPs, practice nurses and cardiologists.

•   National organisations concerned with CHD, professional medical and nursing organisations, and health service training bodies could produce guidelines and training material to increase health professionals' understanding of women's risk of CHD. The issues should also be included in the curricula for medical and nursing training.

•   The professional media also have an important role in increasing the awareness among health care providers of women's risk of CHD.

SMOKING

Smoking is the most important preventable cause of CHD. Women who smoke more than 40 cigarettes a day increase their risk of CHD 20-fold. Policies to reduce smoking among women must include general education measures, social policy measures, and policies specifically related to tobacco.

3   A woman-centred approach to reduce smoking rates is needed, which addresses the girl or woman behind the smoker. It should be supported by social policy measures.

The decline in cigarette smoking rates has been slower among women than among men, and the sex difference in smoking rates has virtually disappeared: by 1992, 28% of women smoked, and 29% of men. Women are also less likely to give up smoking than men (see Chapter 6).

4   Strategies to tackle smoking among women should focus on low-income women, who have the highest rates of smoking, and find it most difficult to give up.

Smoking has become increasingly associated with disadvantage: in 1992, 35% of women in social class V were smokers, compared to 13% in social class I. Strategies to tackle smoking among low-income women should include social policies to support health education measures, with emphasis on the special responsibilities women have at home and at work.

- Action will be needed by government at national and European level, by health promotion agencies, health authorities, and local authorities.

5   Girls and young women should also be a special focus of any strategy to reduce smoking among women.

Girls are now more likely to smoke than boys. Once they have started smoking, they find it more difficult than boys to give up. Over £100 million is spent by under-age children buying cigarettes each year: many will be girls. There is a need for a strategy that addresses personal issues of confidence, self-esteem and weight control; social pressures to smoke; and promotion, price and availability of cigarettes. Schools may need to target girls separately from boys.

- Schools and youth clubs have an important role to play, as well as government, health promotion agencies and retailers.

6　A national ban on tobacco advertising and promotion should be introduced.

A ban on advertising and promotion of tobacco could have an important impact on the number of female smokers. The voluntary agreement is not protecting young women from tobacco advertising.

- The government should support a complete ban.

7　Women's magazines, and other media, should have a tobacco policy which promotes non-smoking and which covers editorial, fashion pages, and advertising.

Millions of women, including young women, are exposed to tobacco advertising in women's magazines. Positive images of women smoking on fashion pages of magazines, in films and on television, reinforce the advertising messages.

8　Women-only smoking cessation courses, led by women, should be provided, to help ensure that the factors sustaining girls' and women's smoking habits are properly addressed.

The majority of women smokers want to give up. Cessation advice for girls and women will be most effective if it is considered in the context of their lives. It could, for example, be linked with stress counselling and women's specific health concerns, such as oral contraception and pregnancy. Dietary advice is also needed when women give up smoking, to address weight control issues.

- The health service, workplaces, and non-government organisations could provide such courses.

PHYSICAL ACTIVITY

Physical activity, including moderate activity such as walking, seems to have a beneficial effect on risk factors for CHD among women, such as HDL-cholesterol levels, high blood pressure, obesity, and adult-onset diabetes (see Chapter 10). However, there is insufficient evidence to conclude that lack of physical activity is an *independent* risk factor for CHD among women. Further longitudinal studies among women are needed.

9   Women's low rates of participation in physical activity and exercise, and the reasons for this, need urgent national attention by government, health promotion organisations, and sports development agencies.

Eight out of ten women fall below the target level of physical activity needed for a health benefit. The proportions are higher among young and middle-aged women. Social class differences in activity levels are also marked: more women in manual social groups – at most risk of CHD – are inactive. A large proportion of women may thus be at increased risk of CHD because of their inactivity.

• National bodies, including the Physical Activity Task Force set up as part of *The Health of the Nation,* should address:

  – the image of sport and the terms used to describe sport, physical activity and exercise
  – the lack of positive female role models
  – transport policy to promote physical activity for women as part of daily routines
  – clear messages about beneficial amounts of exercise
  – new ways to encourage and enable women to increase their levels of physical activity.

Physical activity also needs to be encouraged among women who have CHD, as it can have a positive effect. However, although exercise features strongly in CHD rehabilitation programmes, such programmes often cater more for men, and participation rates are lower, and drop-out rates higher, among women than men.

• Agencies concerned with cardiac rehabilitation should address, and help to improve, women's lower participation in exercise rehabilitation programmes and their higher drop-out rates. Guidelines would be useful.

10 Local authorities should help increase women's levels of physical activity by:

– developing transport policies that promote physical activity as part of a daily routine and provide safe environments, and

– ensuring that leisure and recreation facilities are accessible, affordable and appealing to women.

The focus should be on fitting in physical activity – such as walking and cycling – with normal activities, as part of a daily routine. The social constraints on being physically active – such as street lighting, and safe cycleways – will need to be addressed.

Leisure and recreation facilities which take women's needs into account will enable more women to participate. This could include the provision of creches and transport, for example, and programmes with a wide range of activities, developed in consultation with women.

• Local alliances, including local authorities, health authorities, primary care teams, schools, sports development agencies and the media, could be set up to help improve women's levels of physical activity. Directors of Public Health could take a lead.

11 A long-term education programme, starting among school children, is needed to promote positive attitudes towards physical activity among girls and women.

Children form their attitudes towards physical activity at a very early age and those who exercise regularly in their youth are more likely to be active in later life. A variety of different activities in physical education, which appeal to girls as well as boys, and strategies which enable children to walk or cycle to school, are needed. Positive female role models are also important.

• Schools, local authorities, sports and health promotion agencies, and the media all have a role to play.

DIET

Most policies for improving the nation's diet will apply to both women and men. The national Nutrition Task Force in England, and any equivalent in Scotland, provide a focus for change. Fat consumption is high in women as in men, saturated fat consumption as a percentage of energy is higher in women than men, and women's fruit and vegetable consumption is very low (see Chapter 8).

A primary focus of any strategy to improve diet among women should be poorer women, who eat poorer diets, and it should include social policy measures.

12 National and local strategies to increase fruit and vegetable consumption, particularly among poorer women, need to be introduced.

Although women are increasing their fruit consumption, their vegetable consumption is still very low. The World Health Organization recommends that all adults should eat 400 grams a day: some groups in the UK eat less than half this. There are strong regional and social class differences: expenditure on and consumption of vegetables and fruit is particularly low among poorer groups.

•   The food industry, health promotion agencies, government and the media could help increase fruit and vegetable consumption. Policies at European, national and local level are needed.

13 New strategies are needed to prevent and tackle overweight and obesity among women. Primary prevention of obesity should begin in childhood, with policies to address diet and physical activity.

Obesity is an important determinant of CHD risk in women. As body mass index increases, so does the risk of CHD: even mild to moderately overweight women are at increased risk (see Chapter 8). There has been a large increase in the proportion of overweight and obese women, from 36% in 1986/87 to 45% in 1992. There is a strong inverse relationship between social class and obesity in women. Women with high fat diets also have a higher body mass index.

A high waist:hip ratio seems to increase the risk of CHD. Among women, the waist:hip ratio is lower than among men, but it increases with age. Control of obesity, and increased physical activity, may be particularly important for CHD prevention in South Asian women.

•   The issue of obesity needs to be addressed jointly by the national Task Forces on Nutrition and Physical Activity in England, and equivalent agencies in Scotland, Wales and Northern Ireland.

NATIONAL HEALTH SERVICE

The potential for prevention of CHD among women is greater than for breast cancer or cervical cancer. GPs also have an important role in identifying symptoms of CHD among women.

14 Primary care teams, and well-women clinics, should ensure that women are offered advice on coronary risk reduction, and particularly on smoking.

Combined (overall) risk factor assessment for CHD is important in women as it is in men, and should take age and sex into account. Women should be given information on the health risks of smoking, including the increased risk of smoking and oral contraceptive use. Blood pressure should be measured at least once every five years.

If blood cholesterol levels are measured, they need to be assessed in relation to age and sex, and the threshold for any intervention should be higher for women. The majority of older women have total cholesterol levels above the recommended cut-off points for intervention in men and much of this is accounted for by their higher levels of HDL cholesterol. Over 75% of women aged 55-64 have cholesterol levels over 6.5 mmols/l. For any given cholesterol level, women have a lower risk of CHD than men, at all ages (see Chapter 7). Measuring cholesterol in the absence of other risk factors is not recommended.

15 There is an urgent need for guidelines and advice for primary care teams on appropriate management of risk factors and coronary heart disease in women.

This should include information on the overall risk and presentation of CHD among women, and the implications of sex differences in absolute CHD risk for any given level of a risk factor.

• We are delighted that the British Heart Foundation has issued guidelines for GPs on *Women and the prevention of coronary heart disease* (see Appendix 1).

However, definitive guidelines on the management of high blood cholesterol in healthy women and on the preventive use of HRT must await the results of clinical trials among women. The issue of mass prescription of HRT for reducing CHD risk needs proper discussion. In the meantime, the potential users, and health professionals who write prescriptions, need to be fully informed of the potential benefits, risks and uncertainties.

16 The National Health Service should help increase awareness of women's risk of CHD, among staff and patients, and help to reduce this risk by ensuring that the environment supports healthy choices.

The National Health Service is the UK's largest employer, and women make up 75% of the employees. The NHS could have a role as educator, advocate, and example, to patients and employees, by providing facilities and incentives for physical activity, implementing smoking policies and offering smoking cessation classes, and introducing nutrition policies in canteens.

• The NHS could set an example to other workplaces with a large number of female employees.

17 Health authorities should carry out audits of sex differences in referral rates for CHD, at each stage of the referral pathway. Contracts for CHD services should ensure that women's needs are addressed, including appropriate preventive, diagnostic, treatment and rehabilitation services.

Women are less likely to be referred for diagnostic tests than men, and less likely to receive medical treatment or surgery (see Chapter 4). Audit is needed to determine whether this reflects appropriate clinical practice or not.

• Directors of Public Health could take a lead, and publish results in their annual public health report.

RESEARCH

Most of the research on CHD has been carried out among men and there is a severe dearth of research to inform CHD policies directed at women. It is not always appropriate to extrapolate from findings in men and apply these to women, as some interventions may not have the same effect, either qualitatively or quantitatively. There is a need for more data among women.

18 Research studies among women need to be undertaken on coronary heart disease epidemiology, risk factors, prevention, investigation, treatment, and rehabilitation, to inform policy and interventions.

Such research could include:
– epidemiological studies on risk factors among women
– reasons for high CHD rates among South Asian women, diabetic women, and women in manual social classes

- appropriate interventions and treatment for women (such as cholesterol lowering treatment, hormone replacement therapy, and coronary artery bypass grafting)
- longitudinal studies on physical activity and CHD risk in women
- development and validation of diagnostic tests for CHD in women, and
- reasons for the slower rehabilitation among women.

• National funding agencies, including government and non-government organisations, and academic departments, should make research into CHD among women a priority. Funding agencies could ensure that women are included in any research on CHD.

19 There is a need for further research on the factors affecting health-related behaviour among girls and women, including what motivates them to make changes and to maintain positive health behaviour.

Such research would help inform future prevention strategies, and could include, for example:

- factors affecting the uptake, maintenance, and cessation of smoking, including socioeconomic and domestic factors
- motivation and constraints on physical activity among girls and women
- decision-making and functioning in relation to food choice, in order to influence dietary behaviour, and target advice
- the interrelationships between different health behaviours, such as smoking and weight control, and physical activity and smoking
- the gap between women's perceptions of their own health behaviour and the reality.

• Health promotion agencies, research funding agencies, and health and social researchers should make such research a priority.

20 There is a need for national survey data classifying women's smoking status by their work, economic status and ethnic group, in order to monitor trends and target policies and programmes.

• The government's survey departments, including the Office of Population Censuses and Surveys and the Central Health Monitoring Unit, should ensure that this is undertaken.

21 Research on the benefits and risks of lowering cholesterol levels among healthy women is needed, in order to inform decisions about the management of high cholesterol levels in individual women.

So far, none of the primary prevention trials of cholesterol reduction, using drugs or dietary intervention, have included women and all conclusions on the benefits or risks of intervention among healthy women are based on inference from male data. High levels of HDL cholesterol may be an important protective factor for women.

Definitive guidelines on the treatment of high blood cholesterol among women cannot be drawn up until there is evidence on the benefits of reducing cholesterol levels among women.

• This is an urgent task for research funding agencies and academic researchers.

22 A controlled long-term prospective trial should be undertaken to determine the effects of hormone replacement therapy (HRT) on the risk of coronary heart disease.

Although population studies suggest that among post-menopausal women who take oestrogen, the risk of CHD may be reduced by up to 50%, these studies should be interpreted cautiously. Much of the apparent 'cardioprotective' effect of oestrogen therapy may be attributable to selection bias, and to compliance bias (see Chapter 9). Furthermore, combined HRT (oestrogen and progestogen), which is now more widely prescribed, may have less benefit than oestrogen therapy.

There is insufficient evidence to conclude whether the benefits of combined HRT for cardiovascular risk outweigh the risks of increased breast cancer, and for women and health professionals to make fully informed choices.

• Funding agencies and researchers should undertake studies, including clinical trials, to examine the health benefits and risks of different types of HRT, the effects of different routes of administration, and the appropriate length of treatment.

CHAPTER 4

Attitudes to women and coronary heart disease

IMOGEN SHARP

SUMMARY

Coronary heart disease (CHD) is perceived as a male disease, both by the public and by health professionals. The image is reinforced by the media, health education, research and the medical press. This has several potential implications. Women may be less likely to respond to health messages about CHD if they do not see them as relevant, and less likely to attribute symptoms to CHD. Health professionals may be less likely to offer women advice on CHD prevention and to pick up symptoms at an early stage.

The male image of CHD may also influence patterns of diagnosis and treatment of CHD among women. Studies show that women are less likely to be referred for diagnostic tests such as coronary angiography, and less likely to receive medical treatment or surgery. Furthermore, women tend to be referred at a later stage in the disease process.

Several reasons have been proposed to explain the sex differences in patient care: CHD may be more severe in men; women with cardiac symptoms may be less likely to have true CHD; doctors may perceive sex differences in the predictive value of diagnostic tests; doctors may view treatment as either less effective or more risky among women; or there may be sex differences in patient preferences for tests and treatment. None of these fully explains the sex differences in patient care: there may also be a sex bias in the delivery of medical care.

Women also take longer to recover from CHD than men, and have a worse outcome following a heart attack or cardiac surgery.

There is a clear need for public and professional education to increase awareness of and to address women's risk of CHD.

Coronary heart disease – 'the captain of the men of death' – is typically seen as a male problem, by both the public and health professionals. However, it is also the leading single cause of death among women in the UK, accounting for 23% of women's deaths.

Although most of the deaths from coronary heart disease (CHD) among women are in older age groups, CHD is also the single most common cause of death at younger ages. In 1992, 5,813 women under the age of 65 died from CHD in the UK. This compares with 5,690 deaths from breast cancer, and 902 deaths from cervical cancer in the same age group, both of which attract far more attention.

Women have fewer heart attacks than men but angina is as common in women as in men. For women, angina is most likely to be the presenting complaint of CHD. Thus although women are less likely to die from the disease at younger ages, they are as likely as men of the same age to suffer from the disability associated with angina. Furthermore, although women live longer than men, their extra years of life are often years of disability and dependency: cardiovascular disease (CHD and stroke) is a major contributor.[1]

The male image of CHD victims may affect the attitudes of both the public and professionals. This has several potential implications:

- *Public attitudes*
  Women may be less likely to respond to health messages about CHD if they do not see them as relevant, and less likely to attribute symptoms to CHD.

- *Professional attitudes*
  Health professionals may be less likely to give advice on CHD prevention to women, and less likely to pick up symptoms of CHD at an early stage and to refer women for diagnostic tests and treatment.

- *Recovery from CHD*
  Women may respond less well when they do have heart disease, taking longer to recover, with a worse prognosis.

The male image of the heart attack victim

The media image of a coronary patient is one of a high-powered executive living on his nerves and wedded to his portable telephone. The true heart disease victim is more likely to be a Glasgow labourer, but the image is nevertheless male.[2]

This image permeates not only the mass media but also the scientific community. As long ago as 1892, Osler described the person prone to CHD as "... not the delicate, neurotic person ... but the robust, the vigorous in mind and body, the keen and ambitious man, the indicator of whose engine is always at full speed ahead".[3] Almost 70 years later, in the late 1950s, Friedman and Rosenman described the Type-A or coronary-prone personality as one of "intense striving for achievement, competitiveness, easily provoked impatience, time urgency, abruptness of gesture and speech, overcommitment to vocation or profession, and an excess of drive and hostility":[4] characteristics most typical of an American male executive.

Until recently, the research community has largely neglected women. Most of the studies which underpin understanding and interventions on CHD, including epidemiology, prevention, diagnosis, treatment and rehabilitation, have been carried out in exclusively male populations.[5-10] Research may reinforce the idea that CHD is principally a male concern and this may result in the relative neglect of the condition in women.

The view of CHD as a male disease has also influenced the policy decisions of those involved in health education. Images in much of the health education literature, from the national health education agencies as well as the heart disease charities, have traditionally been primarily male, and men have been the main audience for many publications. Men were also the key target of the government's Look After Your Heart advertising and publicity campaigns.[11] Rarely does health education on CHD show women as victims: women have generally either been ignored altogether,[12] or have been targeted as a means of influencing their partner's risk of CHD, for example by influencing diet.[11, 13]

The medical profession receives similar male images through pharmaceutical advertising for CHD risk-reducing drugs in the medical press.

Implications of the male image of CHD

One of the implications of the image of CHD as a male disease is that women may be less likely to respond to health messages about CHD if they do not see them as relevant, and less likely to recognise symptoms of CHD.

National surveys show that women are less likely than men to see heart disease as a risk to their own health. In a survey carried out by the Health Education Authority in 1990,[14] 52% of women and 65% of men identified heart disease as a possible danger to their own health, although equal proportions recognised CHD as the disease that killed most people (see Table 1). Over nine in ten respondents in both sexes also believe that people can do something to reduce the risk of getting heart disease. Women were more likely to see cancer than CHD as a danger to their own health, possibly reflecting media coverage of women's health problems.

TABLE 1: Public perception of heart disease

Pick out those diseases you think might be a possible danger to your own health:

	Women	Men
Heart disease	52%	65%
Cancer	61%	61%

Which one disease do you think kills most people in Britain today?

	Women	Men
Heart disease	50%	52%
Cancer	43%	41%

n=1,005: 501w/504m

Source: See reference 14.

There are also sex differences in attitudes to risk factors for CHD: women are less likely than men to mention lack of exercise as a risk factor for CHD, but more likely to mention genetics or family history, overweight, and stress as risk factors.[14] Women also appear to feel more guilty about their health behaviour. They are less happy than men that they are doing enough to avoid heart disease in the way that they live, and are more likely to be thinking or trying to do more, particularly with regard to diet. For example, women are more likely than men to report that, when eating out, they choose somewhere which offers a choice of healthy food, and that they usually choose something healthy from the menu[14] (see Table 2).

TABLE 2: Attitudes to risk factors

	Women	Men
DIET		
Choose place which offers healthy foods	51%	35%
Usually pick something healthy from menu	54%	40%
Mainly/only eat healthy foods these days	48%	38%
Don't eat much/never eat fatty or fried foods these days	80%	61%
EXERCISE		
Do physical exercise more than once a week	36%	46%
SMOKING (smokers only)		
Still smoke but definitely intend to stop in near future	18%	14%
Am seriously considering trying to cut down or stop	21%	26%
Eventually would like to cut down or stop	45%	39%
Don't intend to change smoking habits	16%	21%

Source: See reference 14.

Women also tend to believe – not necessarily accurately – that they eat healthily, with 87% reporting that they had 'made healthy changes' or 'mainly or only eat healthy food these days', compared to 78% of men. Women are less likely to report taking regular exercise than men, which concurs with the participation patterns found in the General Household Survey[15] and, more recently, the National Fitness Survey[16] (see Chapter 10). Among smokers, women were more likely to want to give up smoking than men.

Women may also be less likely to recognise symptoms of CHD when they have it, and delay longer in seeking help after the onset of symptoms. For example, studies have found that women take longer to reach hospital when they have a heart attack, perhaps reflecting their lack of awareness of the possibility of a heart attack. They are more likely to call their GP rather than the emergency services when they do have a heart attack, resulting in more delay in reaching hospital.[17] Consistent with this, Framingham data show that women were more likely to have electrocardiogram (ECG) evidence of previously unrecognised heart attacks in routine follow-up visits. Excessive pre-hospital delay can lead to differences in options for treatment.[17, 18]

There is a clear need for public education to increase women's awareness of their risk of CHD, and the possibility of a heart attack.

Professional attitudes to CHD

The male image of CHD may also have major implications for women's health, by influencing the decisions of health professionals. Physicians' perceptions and expectations shape diagnosis, referral for tests and treatment for symptoms.

If health professionals do not see women as potential victims of CHD, they may be less likely to give preventive advice and to offer women risk assessment for CHD. They may also be less likely to diagnose symptoms as CHD in women, and to refer women for relevant tests and treatment.

Furthermore, it is possible that some of the sex differences in CHD morbidity and mortality may be partly attributable to the influence of the male image on diagnostic and coding practices, including assigned cause of death in death certification.[19, 20]

Advice on CHD prevention
Primary care teams have an important opportunity to make women aware of their risk of CHD. However, there are indications that, in primary care, well-women clinics generally focus on the risk of breast and cervical cancer, which affect and kill fewer women than CHD, and that CHD screening clinics tend to be directed at men.[21, 22] It is clearly important that practice nurses, who run the majority of well-person clinics,[21] recognise that CHD is the leading cause

of death in women. However, a 1994 special *Nursing Times* publication on women's health perpetuates the view that CHD is a male disease, and that health promotion clinics for women are primarily for breast and cervical cancer screening. CHD is only discussed briefly in the context of the menopause, and stroke is barely mentioned.[22] If health professionals do not perceive women as at risk of CHD, they may be less likely to offer CHD risk assessment, or to give preventive advice to women.

Diagnosis and management of CHD

The diagnosis and long-term management of CHD have become increasingly dependent on diagnostic tests and invasive procedures (see Table 3).

Several studies have found that, although CHD is the leading cause of death among women, doctors are less likely to refer women for tests and treatment, and CHD in women is likely to be diagnosed later. There is some evidence of a sex bias: doctors are less likely to pursue an 'aggressive' approach to CHD in women than in men. Although much of this research has been carried out in the United States, there is now evidence of a similar pattern in the UK.

Referral for diagnostic tests

Exercise testing, nuclear imaging, cardiac catheterisation with coronary angiography are mainstays of diagnosis (see Table 3). However, several studies have shown that women with angina or myocardial infarction are less likely than men to be referred for diagnostic tests such as exercise testing or angiography, despite more disabling symptoms.

Coronary angiography is the gold standard for establishing a diagnosis of CHD, on the basis of chest pain or angina. However, women are less likely to be referred for angiography than are men with the same diagnosis.[18, 23, 24] For example, in one UK study,[25] women comprised less than a quarter (23%) of patients who were referred with a clinical diagnosis of angina for further investigation by coronary angiography. This sex difference in referral cannot be explained by the prevalence of angina, as angina rates are similar in women and men, but indicates that the threshold for referral of women with chest pain is higher in women than in men.

A study in Northern Ireland hospitals[26] lends further support to these findings. Using routinely available hospital statistics, including over 25,000 episodes of patients discharged from hospital with a diagnosis of CHD, it found that women's rates of invasive investigation – coronary angiography – were five times less than those in men. After controlling for age and admission rates for CHD, there was still a two-fold difference: women's rates were less than half those of men.

These UK findings begin to confirm earlier findings in the United States. Tobin et al,[24] studying the referral decisions on patients suspected of having

TABLE 3: Diagnosis and treatment of CHD

DIAGNOSTIC TESTS

Non-invasive tests

Electrocardiogram (ECG): Electrodes (metal plates) are attached to various parts of the body, to provide a record of the electrical activity of the heart.

Exercise tests: The patient exercises on a treadmill or stationary bicycle. Electrodes are attached to the chest and every three minutes the amount of work being done is increased. During the test an ECG is recorded and a blood pressure obtained every minute.

Nuclear imaging: A radioactive substance is injected, allowing visualisation of the changing pattern of the pool of blood cells within them, or to detect areas of muscle that receive little or no blood.

Invasive tests

Catheterisation: A narrow tube (catheter) is introduced into an artery or vein; the catheter is opaque to X-rays.

Angiography: The catheter is introduced into an artery, and a radio-opaque fluid is injected and an angiogram is displayed on a large video screen. This can show the location of any narrowings in the coronary arteries and whether there are parts of the left ventricle which are not contracting as well as they should.

SURGERY (REVASCULARISATION)

Angioplasty: A specially designed catheter is introduced into an artery through the skin, and advanced to the narrowed coronary artery. Close to the tip of the catheter is an uninflated sausage-shaped balloon which is then inflated at the site of the narrowing so as to stretch the artery and leave it with a wider bore.

Coronary artery bypass sugery (CABG): Narrowings in the coronary arteries are bypassed by inserting a new blood vessel between the aorta and the affected coronary artery beyond the narrowing. Usually, a piece of vein from the patients leg is taken and one end is sewed to the aorta and the other to the coronary artery. Sometimes up to six grafts may be done in one operation.

MEDICAL TREATMENT

Thrombolysis: Thrombolytic drugs are used to dissolve clots in the treatment of heart attacks. They can reduce the risk of death from a heart attack by 25-50%. To be effective, these 'clot-busters' need to be given as soon as possible after the beginning of a heart attack.

Source: See reference 2.

CHD, found that of patients who were positive for CHD on nuclear exercise testing, women were six times less likely than men to be referred for cardiac catheterisation. (A referral for cardiac catheterisation indicates that both the doctor and patient are considering the option of cardiac surgery or angioplasty, rather than drug therapy.)

In this study abnormal nuclear scan results on exercise testing were found in 31% of women and 64% of men with suspected CHD: a two-fold difference. However, among those with abnormal results, 40% of men, but only 4% of women were referred for catheterisation: a 10-fold difference. After controlling for age, previous myocardial infarction, the presence of angina, and abnormal test results, men were more than six times as likely to be referred for catheterisation.

Although women in this study tended to have more frequent symptoms than men (ie more chest pain), doctors were twice as likely to attribute the symptoms of women to non-cardiac causes. This difference was largest among those with abnormal scan results (see Table 4).

TABLE 4: Percentage of symptoms attributed to various causes in patients with suspected CHD, by results of nuclear scan

	Normal		Abnormal	
	Women	**Men**	**Women**	**Men**
Cause	*n=72*	*n=72*	*n=40*	*n=151*
Cardiac	65.3%	77.8%	72.5%	87.4%
Somatic	20.8%	16.7%	15.0%	9.3%
Psychiatric	11.1%	4.2%	12.5%	2.7%
Other, non-cardiac	2.8%	1.4%	0.0%	0.7%

Source: See reference 24.

Referral for treatment

Other research shows a similar pattern, and also indicates that the sex differences in referral for diagnostic tests, such as coronary angiography, are also found in referral rates for treatment for CHD. For individuals undergoing cardiac catheterisation, therapeutic options include medical therapy or cardiac surgery (revascularisation). Several studies in the United States have found that women with CHD have worse access to treatment than men, including thrombolysis, angioplasty and coronary artery bypass surgery (CABG),[18] and a similar pattern is now emerging in the UK.

Ayanian and Epstein,[23] using data on over 80,000 discharges in Massachusetts and Maryland, in the United States, found that women who are hospitalised for CHD undergo fewer major diagnostic and therapeutic procedures than men (see Table 5).

TABLE 5: Rates of referral for angiography and revascularisation

	Massachusetts		Maryland	
	Women	Men	Women	Men
Angiography	16.1%	27.5%	17.7%	28.7%
Revascularisation (coronary artery bypass grafting and angioplasty)	7.4%	15.5%	6.5%	14.1%

Based on: Massachusetts 49,623 discharges
Maryland 33,159 discharges

Source: See reference 23.

Thus men were more likely than women to undergo angiography or revascularisation during hospitalisation for known or suspected CHD, even after adjustment for potential clinical or demographic confounding variables.

Steingart et al[27] also compared the coronary care received by women and men in the United States and found that, although women had angina before their heart attack as frequently as men, and reported greater disability from their symptoms, men were twice as likely as women to undergo cardiac catheterisation and bypass surgery. Patients were included in the study on the basis of a similar cardiovascular event, rather than on the basis of the doctor's decision to recommend a cardiac procedure.

Only 35-50% of women reported no functional limitation with angina, compared to 60-70% of men. However, despite their greater disability from angina, only 15.4% of women were referred for cardiac catheterisation compared to 27.3% of men, and only 5.9% of women were referred for coronary artery bypass surgery, compared to 12.7% of men. Furthermore, women were less likely than men to undergo cardiac catheterisation and bypass surgery (CABG) whether or not they had a previous history of heart attack or angina (see Table 6).

Thus gender was associated with the use of cardiac catheterisation and CABG, and this could not be explained by differences in coronary risk factors or cardiovascular medications. Overall, men were twice as likely to undergo cardiac catheterisation or CABG, even after controlling for other relevant variables such as smoking, education, previous history of diabetes, hypertension and angina. However, bypass surgery was as likely in women as in men once they had undergone cardiac catheterisation.

More recent research indicates that similar sex differences also exist in management of CHD in the UK. For example, Pettigrew et al,[28] examining

TABLE 6: Rates of referral for catheterisation, by previous cardiac history in 112 hospitals in the United States and Canada

	Women	Men
	n=389	*n=1842*
Previous heart attack*	44%	58%
No previous heart attack	5%	9%
Previous history of angina**	44%	64%
No previous history of angina**	6%	15%

*   *p < 0.008*   **   *p < 0.001*

Source: See reference 27.

hospital discharge data from two London regional health authorities (over 23,000 discharges), revealed that in all age groups, and among all patients with a main diagnosis of angina or chronic ischaemia, men were 50%-60% more likely than women to receive surgical treatment, including angioplasty or CABG, in both regions. In North West Thames, where numbers were larger, men with a principal diagnosis of myocardial infarction were also significantly more likely than women to undergo revascularisation (see Table 7). Although there may be sound clinical reasons for these results, such as more severe CHD in men, this is not supported by evidence that women are equally likely to die after a heart attack, after allowance for their older age.

TABLE 7: Women and men undergoing revascularisation (angioplasty or coronary artery bypass surgery)

Principal diagnosis	South West Thames			North West Thames		
	Women	**Men**	**M:F odds ratio**	**Women**	**Men**	**M:F odds ratio**
Myocardial infarction	0.1%	0.7%	7.28*	0.8%	1.9%	2.29
Angina	5.5%	10.4%	1.99	3.4%	7.5%	2.34
Chronic ischaemia	10.7%	18.9%	1.94	21.5%	32.1%	1.73
All cases (after controlling for clinical and demographic confounders)			**1.59**			**1.47**

* few cases: small numbers

Source: See reference 28.

The Yentl syndrome: It is possible that the sex differences in rates of surgical treatment may simply reflect sex differences in referral rates for diagnostic investigation. Several studies have indicated that, once a woman receives a diagnosis of CHD by coronary angiography, there is no sex difference in the likelihood of intervention by revascularisation (CABG or angioplasty).[25, 27] Healy[29] has called this the Yentl syndrome, and proposed that women are only treated like men after coronary angiography has confirmed the presence of CHD.

Thrombolysis: Survival after heart attack has been significantly improved in the past decade by the availability of thrombolytic therapy – the best available treatment after a heart attack. However, studies indicate that women are also less likely than men to receive thrombolysis.[17, 18] This is partly because women (particularly elderly women) are less likely than men of a similar age to be admitted to a coronary care unit[17, 30] where thrombolysis is administered; partly because women take longer to reach hospital after a heart attack,[17, 18] and are thus more likely to be outside the time limit for thrombolysis; and partly due to women's greater age, as many coronary care units have age-related policies on thrombolysis.[31] Once a woman has been admitted to a coronary care unit, there are no sex differences in access to thrombolytic therapy.[17] However, despite more severe heart attacks, patients with the highest mortality – that is, elderly women – are the very people who are not being admitted to coronary care, and are being denied thrombolytic therapy.

In conclusion, studies consistently show a sex difference in patient care for CHD: women undergo potentially useful cardiac procedures less often than men, including diagnostic tests and treatment. Women have angina or chest pain as frequently as men, report more disability from their symptoms, and more disability before a heart attack. However, they are less likely than men to be referred for diagnostic tests (such as coronary angiography), and less likely to receive medical treatment or surgery for CHD, (including thrombolysis, coronary angioplasty, and coronary artery bypass surgery), even after potential confounding factors such as older age are taken into account. Furthermore, women tend to be referred at a later stage in the disease process. Thus women are less likely to undergo procedures that are known (at least in men) to lessen symptoms and improve functional capacity. However, once a diagnosis of CHD has been established by an invasive diagnostic test, the sex difference in treatment for CHD may disappear.

Possible reasons for the sex difference in patient care
Several reasons have been proposed to explain the sex differences in patient care for CHD, and lower rate of use of diagnostic tests and treatment procedures among women.

● *CHD may be more severe in men.*
There may be sound clinical reasons for the sex differences in rates of investigation and treatment if CHD is more severe in men. However, this is not supported by the evidence. Women tend to have more severe CHD at presentation, and more severe heart attacks than men.[17, 30] The prognosis for women with CHD is also at least as severe as in men. Once CHD is clinically manifest, the case fatality rate is greater for women than for men,[23, 32] and women are equally likely to die after heart attack when age is taken into account.[28]

Furthermore, women report more cardiac disability than men before their heart attack. Women with subsequently proved CHD are referred for angiography less often than men, despite their greater disability.

While doctors may perceive CHD as more severe in men, perhaps because of the higher incidence, the evidence does not support sex differences in severity. If they do exist, then this is just as likely to be the result of referral bias.

● *Women with cardiac symptoms may be less likely to have true CHD.*
Angina in women is often associated with normal coronary arteries. Thus, many doctors believe that angina is less likely to be followed by serious cardiovascular events,[33] and are more likely to attribute chest pain in women to non-cardiac causes.[24] For example, one UK study[25] found that of those with angina who underwent angiography, normal coronary arteries were five times more likely in women (41%) than in men (8%). This is in keeping with results in the Coronary Artery Surgery Study (CASS), which found that 50% of women referred with chest pain for angiography had normal coronary arteries or minimal narrowing, compared with only 17% of men[34] (see also page 38).

However, this phenomenon is largely based on findings in younger women, and may not be valid when the analysis includes older women.[27]

Furthermore, the sex difference in the use of cardiac tests and treatment (including angiography and surgery) is found even among those who have had a heart attack – a diagnosis which is well-defined – not simply among those with angina.[23, 28]

● *Doctors may perceive sex differences in the predictive value of diagnostic tests.*
Rates at which diagnostic tests are carried out are likely to be influenced by doctors' perceptions of their value in predicting disease. If tests are perceived as less useful in women than men, doctors are likely to refer women for tests less often. Many non-invasive tests for the evaluation of CHD are believed to be less accurate in women than in men. Exercise testing, for example – an inexpensive, safe technique frequently used in evaluating patients with chest pain – is less accurate in women than in men, and its limitations in predicting CHD in women are well documented.[27, 35] In one UK study, nearly a third of women (29%) with positive exercise tests were found, on angiography, to have

normal coronary arteries, a result similar to that found in other studies.[25] In comparison, only 7% of men with positive exercise tests had normal arteries. The reasons for the sex difference in these 'false positives' are unclear, but misleading results limit the value of exercise testing in women as a screening device.[18] The Rose angina questionnaire has similar problems in predicting disease, but has not been validated among women.

However, sex differences in referral decisions cannot be entirely explained by differences in the performance of diagnostic tests: the diagnostic accuracy of nuclear exercise testing, for example, is similar in women and men when anatomical differences are taken into account.[18, 24]

● *Doctors may view treatment as either less effective or more risky among women.*

Rates at which cardiac procedures are performed are also likely to be influenced by doctors' perceptions of risk and efficacy. If procedures are perceived as more risky or less effective in women than in men, doctors are likely to recommend them less readily for women. Surgeons, for example, may consider that surgery is either less effective or carries greater risk for women. This was supported by some studies during the 1970s and early 80s, which found that women had higher operative mortality[28] and less relief from symptoms after angioplasty and CABG,[23] though long-term survival was equivalent. Early studies explained this by women's smaller arteries, but improvements in surgical techniques may have eliminated that problem.[23, 36] Furthermore, more recent research shows that this higher operative mortality could be the result, rather than the cause, of a referral bias, since women have more advanced disease at the time of referral. However, the perception of higher risk among women may have continued.

● *There may be sex differences in patient preferences for tests and treatment.*

Sex differences in patient preferences could be related to women's own perceptions of the severity of their CHD, and of the benefits and risks of treatment. Women may also be more willing to adapt their lifestyles to avoid surgery: evidence that women are less likely to return to work after a heart attack has been used to support this idea,[23] although this could equally be due to a more negative response to CHD among women (see page 39).

● *There may be a sex bias in the delivery of medical care.*

Neither clinical criteria nor patient preferences seem to explain fully the sex differences in use of tests and treatments for CHD among women and men.

The explanation is likely to arise from the perception that CHD is a male disease, influencing the attitudes of both doctors and patients. The chance of being referred for cardiological tests and treatment depends not only on the patient's clinical presentation, but also on judgements made by health professionals. Doctors may be less likely to offer tests and treatment to women on clinical grounds, or may place less value on the benefits of intervention for women.

The higher incidence of CHD among men at younger ages, prematurely in their economically productive years, means that CHD is more visible among men. Research carried out mainly in male populations, and male images in advertising for cardiovascular drugs in the medical press, for example, may reinforce the idea that CHD is primarily a male concern, and contribute to less 'aggressive' approaches in women.

This could compromise the clinical outcomes in women who undergo procedures at a later stage of disease.

Further research is needed at each stage of the referral pathway – from patient to GP, to cardiologist, to surgeon, to rehabilitation – to determine whether the sex difference in rates of investigation and treatment reflect appropriate clinical practice, and whether procedures are underused in women or overused in men. Further research is also needed to assess the clinical consequences, and whether outcomes in women are compromised by these practices.

The pattern of clinical presentation of CHD seems to differ in women and men. There is also a need for a better means of identifying CHD in women. Some of the standard tests used to determine the likelihood of CHD are of limited value in women. Furthermore, women need to be included in randomised trials for treatment interventions, to assess the effectiveness of procedures in reducing disability among women.

Chest pain but normal arteries: the implications
For patients with chest pain and a diagnosis of normal coronary arteries (most of whom will be women) such a diagnosis may be of little benefit: many patients continue to experience further symptoms and disability. One UK study[25] found that, despite a diagnosis of non-cardiac chest pain, many patients (both women and men) continued to have symptoms and seemed to have derived little benefit from investigation. The vast majority of patients with normal coronary arteries continued to experience chest pain (73% of women and 65% of men), about a third needed further drug treatment for angina (33% of women and 28% of men), and many were readmitted to hospital for chest pain (17% of women and 11% of men).

The implication is that reassurance and counselling is inadequate for patients with chest pain who are found to have normal coronary arteries. In the absence of any other diagnosis, patients may well continue to believe that their pain is cardiac in origin: a situation likely to be perpetuated by the continued prescription of drug treatment for angina. This has obvious consequences for the health service.

The majority of such patients are women. While there is no significant difference in the proportion of women and men continuing to experience symptoms, more women with chest pain have normal coronary arteries.

Recovery and rehabilitation

Recovery from CHD
The male image of CHD may ultimately have an impact on the length and strength of women's recovery, and women may respond less well when they do have heart disease.

Research shows that women take longer to recover from CHD and that the prognosis is worse for women than for men. This has implications both for the women themselves, and also for the health service.

One of the consequences is longer hospital stays, with economic implications for health authorities. Hospital in-patient data show that, on average, women with CHD stay in hospital longer than men at all ages over 65 (see Table 8).[37]

TABLE 8: Hospital in-patient discharges and length of stay for primary diagnosis of CHD, Scotland, 1993

	Discharges		Mean duration of stay (days)	
Age	Women	Men	Women	Men
15-24	10	4	2.0	4.5
25-44	474	1,989	4.0	3.4
45-64	6,244	15,895	4.1	4.2
65-74	5,805	8,640	8.4	5.8
75 and over	6,197	4,420	19.0	11.9
All ages	**18,730**	**30,952**	**10.4**	**5.7**

Source: See reference 37.

Prognosis among women with CHD
One of the reasons for women's slower recovery from CHD is that they have more physical complications, leading to greater morbidity and mortality. Several studies have shown that women fare worse following a heart attack or cardiac surgery, in terms of greater morbidity, more procedural complications and a poorer response to treatment, and greater mortality.[18, 33, 38]

It is well established that women have a worse prognosis after a heart attack than men: they have greater morbidity and are more likely to die. Once CHD is clinically manifest, the case fatality rate for women is greater than that for men, and in particular, women seem to be at increased risk of reinfarction and death after a heart attack.[18] For example, one UK study found that one-third of women admitted to hospital with a heart attack had died within six months, compared to one-sixth of men.[39] Only part of this excess risk may be explained by older age, greater prevalence of risk factors such as hypertension and diabetes, and greater severity of heart attack among women. Women of all ages are more likely to die following heart attack than are comparably aged men. Some of the excess risk may also be due to sex differences in treatment.[18]

Women also have less relief from symptoms and a higher risk of death than men after clinical procedures such as bypass surgery and angioplasty, a consistent finding for over 15 years.[18, 36, 38, 40] This includes higher operative mortality, and lower long-term survival. For example, one 1992 study found that the death rate in hospital after first bypass surgery was four times greater among women than men.[41] The higher mortality after bypass surgery may relate partly to differences in the prevalence among women of risk factors for death: women are more likely to be older, to have diabetes or hypertension, have a smaller body size, and have smaller coronary arteries.[36, 40] However, one important reason for the higher mortality after surgery may also be women's referral for procedures at a more advanced stage of CHD.[42] For example, Kahn[38] found that women's higher procedural mortality is independently predicted not by gender but by two traits more common in women: older age and New York Heart Association Class IV angina at baseline, indicating greater severity.

Thus women in studies of cardiac surgery tend to be older and sicker than the men, and may have had surgery with more advanced CHD. It has been suggested that late referral for angioplasty and CABG may compromise the safety of these procedures for women. However, what constitutes 'appropriate' referral is unclear, given the high prevalence of risk factors among women. It is also unclear whether any delay is due to the clinical features of the disease in women, or due to health care delivery factors.[36]

Rehabilitation among women

Rehabilitation after CHD, including psychosocial adjustment, seems to be slower for women. This may also lead to longer stays in hospital. If women's heart attacks are perceived as being more serious, both by themselves and by the medical staff, they may get treated more cautiously by staff, and may recover more slowly. Furthermore, the women themselves may be more anxious, and reluctant to prepare for early discharge from hospital.

Cardiac rehabilitation programmes can aid recovery and provide valuable secondary prevention after a heart attack, and can decrease death rates. However, women are less likely than men to take part in a structured rehabilitation programme after a heart attack, particularly those involving vigorous exercise.[43] They are also more likely to drop out of such a programme prematurely. Oldridge, for example, found a one-year drop-out rate of 64% among women, and 42%

among men patients after heart attack or cardiac surgery.[44]

The issue of physical and social rehabilitation, and of the psychological effects of CHD on women, has been relatively neglected in research until recently. In particular, there has been very little research carried out among women on the psychosocial experience of having a heart attack.

The small-scale studies that have included women indicate that women suffer more distress and psychological disturbance than men following heart attack, and more difficulty in rehabilitation, in both the short and the long term.[45, 46, 47]

It is well recognised that stress is an important factor in determining the success of rehabilitation in CHD.[2] Psychological rehabilitation problems may be more related to attitudes that patients form in the period immediately after their heart attack and their pre-existing psychological status than to the severity of the heart attack.[45] For example, one study[48] found that, four days after a heart attack, women were more likely to report depression, negative self-image, and poor coping mechanisms. Another study showed significantly higher levels of anxiety in women than in men admitted to a British coronary care unit. High anxiety levels were linked with fatal heart attacks prior to discharge.[49]

In the longer term, women heart attack patients also experience more limited social functioning, and more psychological, emotional and physical symptoms than men, after controlling for age and morbidity.[30] Women also return to work later than men following a heart attack.[45]

Following a review of the literature, Shaw[45] suggests that women's less favourable recovery following heart attack may be related to the strength of sex role orientation. The more feminine women experienced greater anxiety and were slower to resume normal activities, perhaps because the illness affected their self-image more.

Thus the research that has been carried out so far on the experiences of women following CHD suggests that women adapt less well than men, have more difficulty in rehabilitation, and have different needs and problems than men. Health professionals may be badly placed to meet these needs. Larger studies are much needed to establish the reasons for the slower rehabilitation among women, and how to deal with it.

Lack of caring partner

One further reason for longer stays in hospital – and slower rehabilitation – among women at all ages over 65 may be that women are less likely to have a caring partner at home to look after them. Men's life expectancy is lower, and thus women are more likely than men to be widowed and alone when they have CHD. As a result, they are may be discharged from hospital later: the hospital providing care as well as cure.

Conclusion

The male image of CHD may have an important impact on women's health, by affecting the way CHD risk and symptoms are perceived and dealt with, both by women themselves and by health professionals. The impact is apparent at every stage, from prevention, to diagnosis, to treatment, to rehabilitation.

Despite the fact that CHD is also the leading cause of death among women, almost all the studies of CHD have been among men. CHD accounts for almost a quarter of all deaths among women, and angina is as common in women as in men. However, much less is known about CHD in women, about its clinical progress, and about women's responses to the disease.

CHD becomes clinically manifest at a later stage in the life of women. The UK has an increasingly ageing population, and about two-thirds of retired people are women. A 23% increase in the 65-79s and a 45% increase in the over 80s is expected between 1988 and 2025: most will be women.

As the proportion of older women in the population increases, so the incidence of CHD will increase. Women's extra years of life may be years of disability, and cardiovascular diseases - including CHD and stroke - are an important cause. The implications for the health service, as well as for women themselves, are obvious. The need for preventive strategies, diagnostic tests, and treatment and rehabilitation policies which address women's needs is apparent.

There is a clear need for public and professional education, to increase awareness of women's risk of CHD, and the possibilities for prevention, diagnosis, and treatment.

References

1   Royal College of Physicians 1991. *Preventive medicine: a report of a working party of the Royal College of Physicians*. London: Royal College of Physicians of London.
2   Julian D, Marley C. 1991. *Coronary heart disease: the facts*. Oxford: Oxford University Press.
3   Osler W. 1892. *Lectures on angina and allied states*. New York: Appleton.
4   Friedman M, Rosenman RH. 1959. Association of specific overt behaviour pattern with blood and cardiovascular findings: blood cholesterol level, blood clotting time, incidence of arcus senilis and clinical coronary artery disease. *Journal of the American Medical Association;* 169: 1286-1296.
5   MRFIT Research Group. 1982. Multiple Risk Factor Intervention Trial: risk factor changes and mortality results. *Journal of the American Medical Association*; 248: 1465-1477.
6   Shaper AG, Pocock SJ, Walker M, Cohen NM, Wale CJ, Thomson AG. 1982. British Regional Heart Study: cardiovascular risk factors in middle-aged men in 24 towns. *British Medical Journal*; 283: 179-186.
7   Marmot MJ, Rose G, Shipley M, Hamilton PJS. 1978. Employment grade and coronary heart disease in British civil servants. *Journal of Epidemiology and Community Health*; 32: 244-249.

8   Hjerman J, Byre KV, Holme I, Leren P. 1981. Effect of diet and smoking intervention on the incidence of coronary heart disease: report from the Oslo Study Group of a randomised trial in healthy men. *Lancet*; 2: 1303-1310.

9   Lipid Research Clinics Program. 1984. The Lipid Research Clinics Coronary Primary Prevention Trial results. I. Reduction in incidence of coronary heart disease. *Journal of the American Medical Association*; 251: 351-364.

10 WHO European Collaborative Group. 1980. Multifactorial trial in the prevention of coronary heart disease. Recruitment and initial findings. *European Heart Journal*; 1: 73-80.

11 Health Education Authority. 1992. *Look After Your Heart! Report on the first four years of advertising and publicity for the 'Look After Your Heart' programme: 1987-1990.* London: Health Education Authority.

12 Amos A. 1993. In her own best interests? Women and health education: a review of the last fifty years. *Health Education Journal*; 52: 140-150.

13 Farrant W, Russell J. 1986. *The politics of health information: 'Beating heart disease' as a case study in the production of Health Education Council publications.* Bedford Way Papers 28. London: University of London Institute of Education.

14 Health Education Authority. 1990. Heartbeat: an evaluation of the 'Look After Your Heart'publicity campaign. Trend volume: November 1990. Research carried out by British Market Research Bureau on behalf of the Health Education Authority.

15 Office of Population Censuses and Surveys. *General household surveys.* London: HMSO.

16 Activity and Health Research. 1992. *Allied Dunbar National Fitness Survey*: a report on activity patterns and fitness levels. Commissioned by the Sports Council and Health Education Authority. London: Sports Council and Health Education Authority.

17 Clarke KW, Gray D, Keating NA, Hampton JR. 1994. Do women with acute myocardial infarction receive the same treatment as men? *British Medical Journal*; 309: 563-566.

18 Hsia J. 1993. Gender differences in dignosis and management of coronary disease. *Journal of Women's Health*; 2 (4): 349-352.

19 Stehbens WE. 1987. An appraisal of the epidemic rise of coronary heart disease and its decline. *Lancet*; 1: 606-611.

20 Bartley M. 1985. Coronary heart disease and the public health 1850-1983. *Sociology of health and illness*; 7; 3: 289-313.

21 Calnan M, Williams S. 1992. *Coronary heart disease prevention: the role of the general practitioner. Final report of a national study commissioned by the Department of Health with the Health Education Authority.* Canterbury: University of Kent.

22 Nursing Times. 1994. *Women's health: a Nursing Times special publication.* London: Macmillan Magazines Ltd.

23 Ayanian JZ, Epstein AM. 1991. Differences in the use of procedures between women and men hospitalised for coronary heart disease. *New England Journal of Medicine*; 325: 4: 221-225.

24 Tobin JN, Wassertheil-Smoller S, Wexler JP, Steingart RM, Budner N, Lense L, Wachspress J. 1987. Sex bias in considering coronary bypass surgery. *Annals of Internal Medicine*; 107: 19-25.

25 Sullivan KS, Holdright DR, Wright CA, Sparrow JL, Cunningham D, Fox KM. 1994. Chest pain in women: clinical, investigative and prognostic features. *British Medical Journal*: 308: 883-6.

26 Kee F, Gaffney B, Currie S, O'Reilly D. 1993. Access to coronary catheterisation: fair shares for all? *British Medical Journal*; 307: 1305-1307.

27 Steingart RM, Packer M, Hamm P et al. 1991. Sex differences in the management of coronary artery disease. *New England Journal of Medicine*; 325: 4: 226-230.

28 Pettigrew M, McKee M, Jone J. 1993. Coronary artery surgery: are women discriminated against? *British Medical Journal*; 306: 1164-1166.

29 Healy B. 1991. The Yentl syndrome. *New England Journal of Medicine*; 325: 274-276.

30 Wiklund I, Herlitz J, Johansson S, Bengtson A, Karlson BW, Persson NG. 1993. Subjective symptoms and well-being differ in women and men after myocardial infarction. *European Heart Journal*; 14: 1315-1319.

31 Hannford PC, Kay CR, Ferry S. 1994. Agism as explanation for sexism in provision of thrombolysis. *British Medical Journal*; 309: 573.

32 Lerner DJ, Kannel WB. 1986. Patterns of coronary heart disease morbidity and mortality in the sexes: a 26-year follow-up of the Framingham population. *American Heart Journal*; 111: 383-390.

33 Wenger NK. 1990. Gender, coronary artery disease, and coronary bypass surgery. *Annals of Internal Medicine*; 112: 557-558.

34 Kennedy JW, Killip T, Fisher LD, Alderman EL, Gillespie MJ, Monk MB. 1982. The clinical spectrum of coronary artery disease and its surgical and medical management, 1974-1979. The coronary artery surgery study. *Circulation*; 66 (suppl 3): 16-23.

35 Sketch MN, Mohiuddin SM, Lynch JD, Zencka AE, Runco V. 1975. Significant sex differences in the correlation of electrocardiographic exercise testing and coronary arteriograms. *American Journal of Cardiology*; 36: 169-173.

36 Weintraub WS, Wenger NK, Jones EL, Craver JM, Guyton RA. 1993. Changing clinical characteristics of coronary surgery patients: differences between men and women. *Circulation*; 88 (2): 79-86.

37 Information and Statistics Division, National Health Service in Scotland. 1994. *Scottish Health Statistics 1993*. Edinburgh: Common Services Agency.

38 Khan SS, Nessim S, Gray R, Czer LS, Chaux A, Matloff J. 1990. Increased mortality of women in coronary artery bypass surgery: evidence for referral bias. *Annals of Internal Medicine*; 112: 561-567.

39 Wilkinson P, Laji L, Ranjadayalan K, Parsons L, Timmis AD. 1994. Acute myocardial infarction in women: survival analysis in first six months. *British Medical Journal*; 309: 566-569.

40 Rahimtoola SH, Bennett AJ, Grunkemeier GL, Block P, Starr A. 1993. Survival at 15 to 18 years after coronary bypass surgery for angina in women. *Circulation*; 88 (2): 71-78.

41 Zehr KJ, Chang A, Siu C, Kumar P, Baumgartner WA, Chandra NC. 1994. Gender determines survival from coronary bypass surgery. *Journal of the American College of Cardiology*; 57: 347A.

42 Kornfield J. 1991. Coronary disease in women. *Cardio*; August 1991: 5.

43 McGee HM, Horgan JH. 1992. Cardiac rehabilitation programmes: are women less likely to attend? *British Medical Journal*; 305: 283-284.

44 Oldridge MB, Lasalle D, Jones NL. 1980. Exercise rehabilitation of female patients with coronary heart disease. *American Heart Journal*; 338: 1366-1367.

45 Shaw DG. 1990. *Gender and heart disease – is there a difference? A study of the possible relationship between gender and the psychological impact of heart attack*. MSc research project: City University. Unpublished. (This thesis has provided a useful overview of the literature on sex differences in the psychological impact of heart attacks.)

46 Stern MJ, Pascale L, Ackerman A. 1977. Life adjustment post myocardial infarction. *Archives of Internal Medicine*; 137: 1680-1685.

47 Sharpe PA, Clark NM, Janz NK. 1991. Differences in the impact and management of heart disease between older women and men. *Women and Health*; 17: 25-43.

48 Guiry E, Conroy RM, Hickey N, Mulcahy R. 1987. Psychological response to an acute coronary event and its effects on subsequent rehabilitation and lifestyle change. *Clinical Cardiology*; 10: 256-260.

49 Vetter NJ, Cay EL, Philip AE, Stranger RE. 1977. Anxiety on admission to the coronary care unit. *Journal of Psychosomatic Research*; 21: 73-78.

CHAPTER 5

Coronary heart disease in women

The scale of the problem: should we be concerned?

KAY-TEE KHAW AND IMOGEN SHARP

SUMMARY

Coronary heart disease (CHD) is the leading cause of death among women in the UK, accounting for almost a quarter of women's deaths, or about 76,000 deaths annually. It is also a major cause of ill health in women. Angina is as common in women as men.

Women's CHD death rates in the UK are among the highest in the world. Women aged 35-74 in Scotland have CHD death rates ten times those among women in Japan. Also, women in countries with the highest CHD death rates have higher rates than men in low rate countries. The decline in CHD death rates over the last decade has been slower among women than men.

Women have lower CHD rates than men. Biological and lifestyle reasons are proposed: women may be biologically 'more resistant' to CHD (with higher levels of 'protective' HDL cholesterol, and protection from oestrogen), and have traditionally more healthy lifestyles (such as lower smoking rates).

Most CHD research has been carried out among men, but it is not always appropriate to apply the findings to women. Even if the relative benefits of interventions are similar in both sexes, absolute benefits will be lower for women as they have lower rates of CHD, and different decisions may need to be made.

International comparisons indicate that the same environmental factors are operating in both sexes, so preventive interventions aimed at the general population are likely to be effective for both.

Mortality

Coronary heart disease (CHD) has traditionally been perceived as a disease of men. However, it is also the leading single cause of death among women in the UK, accounting for almost a quarter (23%) of all deaths among women (see Figure 1). Annually, approximately 76,000 women and 90,000 men die of CHD in the UK.[1]

FIGURE 1: Main causes of death in women of all ages in the UK, 1992

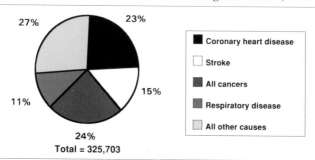

Source: see reference 1.

CHD rates increase with age in both sexes, but at younger ages, men have much higher rates (see Figure 2). This has diverted attention from the fact that CHD is also the largest killer in women.

Among women, death rates from diseases of the cardiovascular system are greater than those from all other major causes. CHD is responsible for the deaths of more women than breast cancer or cervical cancer, both in under-65 year olds, and in older age groups (see Table 1). Myocardial infarction – or heart attack – accounts for over half of all deaths from CHD, among both women (56%) and men (57%). Because women live longer than men on average, they are also more likely to die of CHD eventually at a very old age.

TABLE 1: Deaths among women in the UK, 1992

	All ages		< 75 years		< 65 years	
	n	%	n	%	n	%
Ischaemic heart disease	76,364	23.4	21,841	20.6	5,813	13.1
Breast cancer	15,221	4.7	9,275	8.8	5,690	12.8
Cervical cancer	1,863	0.6	1,368	1.3	902	2.0

% refers to percentage of total deaths in that age group

Source: See reference 1.

FIGURE 2: Main causes of deaths in older women and men, by age, UK, 1992

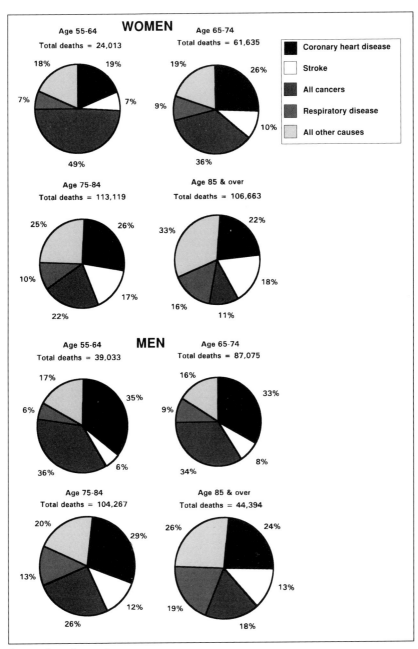

FIGURE 3: Hospital in-patients and day cases* among women, by selected condition and age, England, 1990/91

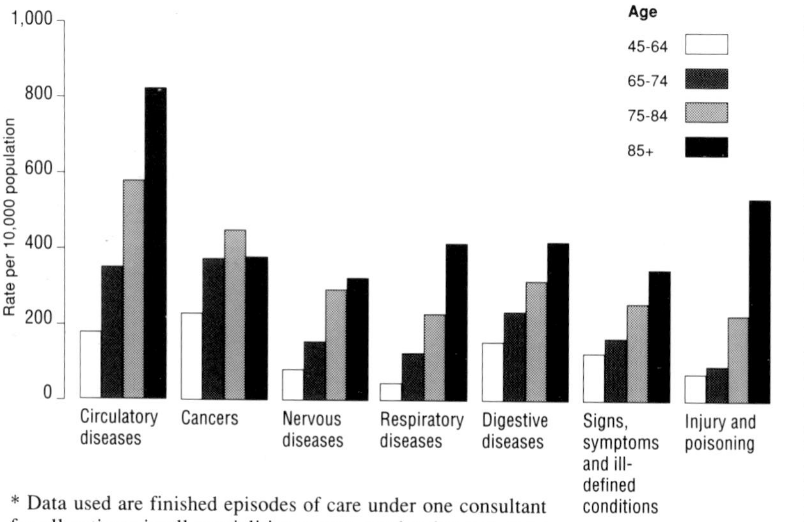

* Data used are finished episodes of care under one consultant for all patients in all specialities except regular day and night cases and maternity patients using delivery facilities only.

Source: See reference 2.

Morbidity

CHD is also a major cause of morbidity (illness) and disability in women. Among older women circulatory diseases, including CHD and stroke, are the leading cause of hospital admissions[2] (see Figure 3) and are also the major reason for GP consultations,[3] which act as a marker for morbidity, disability and loss of quality of life.

The Health Survey for England 1992[4] found that 25% of women have ever had a cardiovascular disorder, (including heart attack, stroke, angina, hypertension, diabetes and other heart trouble). Angina is as common in women as in men, and is the most common form of presentation of CHD among women. Overall, an estimated 900,000 women in the UK suffer from angina.[4,5] Although myocardial infarction (heart attack) may be less common in women than men, painless myocardial infarction is common, particularly in older ages. Furthermore, while women live longer than men, their extra years of life are often years of disability, and cardiovascular diseases (including CHD and stroke) make a major contribution.

International differences

Marked regional variations, both internationally and within the UK, indicate that there is considerable scope for reducing CHD rates among women.

Death rates for CHD among women in the UK are among the highest in the world (see Figure 4). International comparisons of rates show a league table ranking that is similar for both men and women. Thus countries with high rates of CHD among women also have high rates among men, suggesting that environmental determinants affect women and men similarly, and that preventive interventions which are targeted towards the general population are likely to be effective for both. The influence of such environmental factors far outweighs the magnitude of any sex differences within each population.

FIGURE 4: Death rates from CHD, women and men aged 35-74, 1991, selected countries

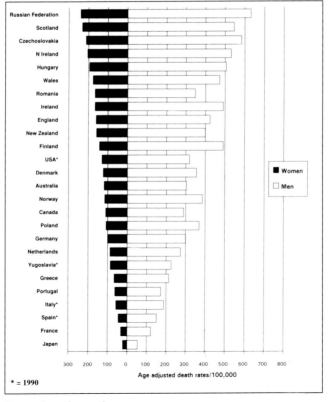

* = 1990

Source: See reference 5.

There is a 10-fold international variation in CHD death rates among women. Women aged 35-74 in Scotland (where the rate is 233 deaths per 100,000 women) have a risk of CHD that is more than 10 times higher than women of the same age in Japan (22 per 100,000).[5]

International comparisons also reveal that, while women have lower rates of CHD than men within countries, women in countries at the top of the international league table have rates which are far higher than men in the low rate countries at the bottom (see Figure 4). Thus a 35-74 year old woman in Scotland (where the death rate for CHD is 233 per 100,000 women) or Northern Ireland (197 per 100,000) is about four times more likely to die from CHD than a man in the same age group in Japan (55 deaths per 100,000 men).

Regional differences

Within the UK, for women as well as for men, there are marked regional differences in CHD rates. CHD death rates are highest among women in the North of England, Scotland and Northern Ireland, and lowest in the South of England and East Anglia. There is a two-fold difference in CHD death rates between different regional health authorities, among women under 75 years.[6] Variations between district health authorities are greater. Within England, for example, there are four-fold differences in CHD death rates among women under 65: the rate in Cambridge district is 11.5 per 100,000, compared to 48 per 100,000 in Rochdale.[6]

Women in regions with high rates of CHD have age adjusted rates which are higher than those of men in regions with low rates: 324 per 100,000 among women in the North of England, compared to 288 per 100,000 among men in East Anglia.[5]

Time trends

CHD death rates in the UK have been falling since the late 1970s. However, the decline among both women and men in the UK has been slower than that in other similar developed countries, such as the United States, Canada and Australia.

Furthermore, death rates from CHD have fallen more slowly among UK women than among men (see Figure 5). Between 1981 and 1991, for example, CHD death rates fell by only 17% among women in England, but by 25% among men. In Scotland they fell by 20% among women, and 23% among men. In Wales, the corresponding falls were 21% among women and 26% among men. In some countries, such as Japan, France and Ireland, declines in CHD death rates have been faster among women than men.

FIGURE 5: Reductions in death rates from CHD, women and men aged 35-74, between 1981 and 1991, selected countries

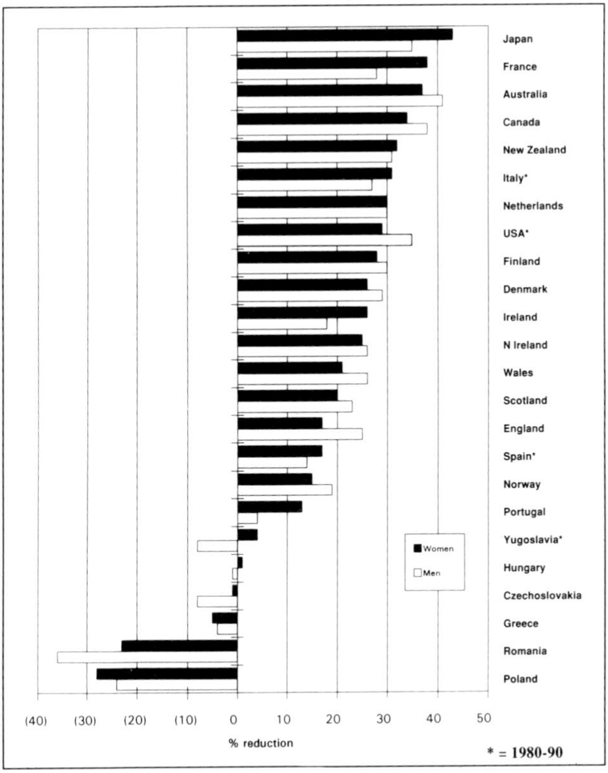

Source: See reference 5.

Possible reasons for the sex differences in CHD rates

Both biological and lifestyle (behavioural) reasons have been proposed for the sex differences in CHD rates. Women may be biologically 'more resistant' to CHD than men; and men may be more likely to behave in ways that confer CHD risk.

Biological factors

There is some disagreement about whether the risk factors for CHD are similar in women and men. However, data from the Framingham study[7] suggest that the relative risks associated with the classic risk factors – blood pressure, blood cholesterol and cigarette smoking – are similar for both sexes: so biologically they confer the same magnitude of risk in relative terms (see Table

2). Thus a woman who smokes, or has a high blood cholesterol level, has a greater risk of CHD than a woman who does not.

TABLE 2: Relative risks* for CHD in Framingham women and men, 1977-79, four-year follow-up

Factor	Relative risk	
	Women	**Men**
Systolic blood pressure	1.4	1.6
Total cholesterol	1.4	1.4
HDL cholesterol	0.5	0.5
Cigarette smoking	1.2	1.1

* Comparison of 80th vs. 20th percentile for risk factor; smoker versus non-smoker

Source: See reference 7.

Some of the sex differences in CHD may be due to higher prevalence of classic risk factors – high blood cholesterol and hypertension – among men. At younger ages, women in the UK have lower levels of blood cholesterol and blood pressure. After middle age, at around the time of the menopause, however, they increase more sharply among women than among men, and the prevalence of hypertension and high blood cholesterol is much greater in older women than older men (see Chapter 7).

Nevertheless, even though the relative risks associated with classical risk factors may be similar in women and men, the absolute risks appear to be lower. Women have CHD rates between three and five times lower than those of men. After adjusting for sex differences in total blood cholesterol and blood pressure, a two-fold sex difference in CHD risk still remains.[8, 9] The main biological reasons proposed are women's higher average levels of the protective HDL cholesterol, and the protection afforded by oestrogen.

Thus, data from the Framingham study show that a 'high risk' woman – that is a woman who has all the classic risk factors – has the same risk of CHD as an 'average risk' man. 'High risk' women, however, have higher rates of CHD events than 'low risk' men – that is men with no risk factors.

However, even though HDL cholesterol and oestrogen may help explain the sex differences in CHD, they do not explain the large international differences. For example, women in Japan have the lowest rates of CHD internationally, but they also have low HDL levels and low oestrogen levels. Migration studies indicate that these are not simply due to genetic factors: Japanese women living in the United States have higher rates of CHD, closer to those of white women in the United States.

Lifestyle factors

Some of the sex difference in CHD rates may also be due to men's traditionally more unhealthy lifestyles. They have tended to smoke more and eat less fruit and vegetables. Lack of physical activity has traditionally been the only behavioural risk factor more prevalent among women than men. However, the sex differences in behavioural risk factors are now changing, as men have become more aware of the risk of CHD and have changed their lifestyles in response. Women, in contrast, are adopting the traditional lifestyles of men. For example, women's rates of smoking are declining at a much slower rate than men's, and the sex difference in smoking has now virtually disappeared. In Glasgow, it has reversed: among 25-34 year olds, some 50% of women smoke, compared to 40% of men. The changing patterns of smoking rates among girls and women may lead to increased rates of CHD among women in the future.

Lack of research data on CHD among women

Most of the research into the causes, prevention and treatment of CHD has been carried out among men, mainly due to the well-recognised excess of incidence of CHD among men in younger groups, and the easier accessibility of populations of men for study, for example via the workplace. There is a dearth of data in women, and this is a cause for real concern.

While biological plausibility may suggest that what works in men is also likely to work in women, it may not always be appropriate to extrapolate from findings in men and apply those findings to women. Some interventions may not have the same effect either qualitatively or quantitatively including, for example, coronary artery bypass grafting, dietary intervention, and cholesterol-lowering therapy. There is a need for more data on the effects of such interventions in women, and others such as hormone replacement therapy. An inadequate understanding of the process of CHD in women may result in inappropriate interventions.

Implications for intervention

Even if the relative benefits or risks of treatment are the same in women as men, the absolute benefit of the treatment will be very different, simply because women have lower rates of CHD than men.

Table 3 illustrates this point. Results from lipid-lowering drug trials in men indicate that treatment of high cholesterol may reduce CHD mortality by 20%.[10] Assuming the same relative risks for high cholesterol in both women and men, and the same benefit from treatment across both sexes and all ages, Table 3 gives estimates of the number of people with cholesterol levels over

6.5 mmol/l, in each age and sex group, who would need to be treated to prevent one CHD death. The absolute benefit depends on the incidence of CHD (for which age and sex are important determinants) as well as the prevalence of the risk factor in each group.

TABLE 3: Estimated numbers of people with cholesterol levels ≥6.5 mmol/l treated for five years to prevent one CHD death within five years (England and Wales)*

Ages	35-44	45-54	55-64
Women	4,649	1,112	315
Men	862	234	104

*assuming similar benefits from treatment in all age and sex groups

Source: See reference 11.

This illustrates that completely different decisions may need to be made about the values of the risk-benefit balance of intervention in women compared to men. However, it also highlights the lack of research data on the benefits and risks of lowering cholesterol levels among women.

However, it is important to compare the benefits of screening women for CHD risk factors with the benefits of existing national screening programmes for women, for example for breast and cervical cancer. Among women aged 50-64 years in England and Wales, CHD is the leading single cause of death, killing more women than either breast cancer or cervical cancer. The potential for prevention of CHD is far greater than for breast cancer and cervical cancer in real terms. Fewer women would need to be screened and treated to prevent one event.

Thus, although the potential benefit of screening programmes for CHD may be less for women than for men, it is nevertheless no worse than for current screening programmes for breast cancer and cervical cancer that are considered worthwhile.

Conclusion

There is clearly no room for complacency. It must be recognised that CHD is the leading cause of mortality and morbidity among women in the UK. The UK is now among countries with the highest CHD rates in the world, in women as well as men. The differences in CHD rates between countries far outweigh the sex differences within countries, and international differences in rates among women closely parallel those among men. The same environmental or behavioural factors that relate to the high rates seem to be operating in both sexes, and thus preventive interventions targeted towards the general population are likely to be effective for both. There is an overwhelming potential for reducing the very high risk of CHD among women in the UK, which needs to be addressed.

This section is based on a paper prepared for the National Forum for Coronary Heart Disease Prevention by Professor Kay-Tee Khaw, Professor of Clinical Gerontology, University of Cambridge. Professor Khaw is an individual member of the Forum.

References

1   Office of Population Censuses and Surveys. 1993. *Mortality statistics 1992: Cause. England and Wales*. Series DH2, no 19. London: HMSO.
    Registrar General Scotland. 1993. *Annual report 1992*. Edinburgh: General Register Office.
    Registrar General Northern Ireland. 1993. *Annual report 1992*. Belfast: General Register Office.

2   Department of Health. 1994. *Hospital episode statistics England: financial year 1990-1991*. London: Department of Health.

3   Office of Population Censuses and Surveys. 1986. *Morbidity statistics from general practice, 1981-82, third national survey*. Series MB5, no 1. London: HMSO.

4   Breeze E, Maidment A, Bennett N, Flatley J, Carey S. 1994. *Health survey for England 1992. A survey carried out by the Social Survey Division of OPCS on behalf of the Department of Health*. London: HMSO.

5   Rayner M. 1994. Coronary heart disease statistics. *British Heart Foundation/Coronary Prevention Group statistics database*. London: British Heart Foundation. 1994.

6   Department of Health. 1993. *Public health common data set 1993*. Surrey: Institute of Public Health, University of Surrey.

7   Castelli WP, Garrison RJ, Wilson PWF et al. 1986. Incidence of coronary heart disease and lipoprotein cholesterol levels: the Framingham study. *Journal of the American Medical Association*; 256: 2835-2838.

8   Isles CG, Hole DJ, Hawthorne VM, Lever AF. 1992. Relation between coronary risk and coronary mortality in women of the Renfrew and Paisley survey: comparison with men. *Lancet*; 339: 702-706.

9   Wingard DL, Suarez L, Barrett-Connor E. 1983. The sex differential in mortality from all causes and ischaemic heart disease. *American Journal of Epidemiology*; 117: 165-172.

10 Tyroler HA. 1989. Overview of clinical trials of cholesterol lowering in relationship to epidemiologic studies. *American Journal of Medicine*; 87 (supplement 4A): 14-19S.

11 Khaw KT, Rose G. 1989. Cholesterol screening programmes: how much benefit? *British Medical Journal*; 299: 606-607.

CHD risk among women:
Whitehall II and other studies

MICHAEL MARMOT AND E J BRUNNER

SUMMARY

At younger ages, women have lower coronary heart disease (CHD) mortality rates than men, but the sex difference reduces after about age 50. Women in manual social classes have much higher CHD rates than women in non-manual groups: the gap is wider than among men, and seems to be increasing. The Whitehall II study also shows greater morbidity – angina and ECG ischaemia – in women in lower employment grades. Although angina is as common in women as in men in the study, women with angina are less likely to have ECG abnormalities.

Women with a family history of CHD, especially those whose parents died at a younger age, have an increased risk of CHD.

The major risk factors for CHD – smoking, high blood cholesterol and hypertension – are the same in both sexes, but operate at different levels. Women who smoke over 40 cigarettes a day increase their CHD risk 20-fold. Social class differences in CHD among women are not reflected in total cholesterol or blood pressure levels. However, women in lower employment grades do have a worse lipid profile (lower HDL cholesterol, higher LDL cholesterol and a worse LDL:HDL ratio), and higher smoking rates. Hypertension is common among older women, which is important in an ageing population.

Obesity, and high waist:hip ratio, increase the risk of CHD. Body mass index shows an inverse social class gradient, which is stronger in women than men. Higher waist:hip ratios among women in manual groups may help explain their higher CHD rates.

Diabetes increases the risk of CHD, and imposes a greater risk of CHD in women than in men. South Asian women also have a particularly high risk of CHD: 50% higher than other UK women, which is probably due to the insulin resistance syndrome. Afro-Caribbean women have relatively low rates of CHD.

Understanding of the predictors of coronary heart disease (CHD) comes mainly from studies of middle-aged white men. To some extent this is due to the fact that, among under-65 year olds, CHD is more common in men than women. Prospective studies have produced little evidence that the mechanism of CHD is different in women and men, implying that the principal risk factors have a similar meaning for both sexes.

It is often pointed out that the sex difference in CHD rates narrows after the menopause, giving rise to speculation that being pre-menopausal is in some way protective for women, and that being post-menopausal is harmful, which may be the case. However, national CHD mortality statistics indicate that this narrowing of the sex difference is due to a slowing down in the increase in CHD rates among men after about age 50, rather than an acceleration in female rates. CHD rates among women continue to rise steadily, with no inflection at the time of menopause, but male rates rise less steeply at older ages (see Figure 1). National mortality data therefore suggest that it may be the loss of a harmful factor in men rather than the loss of a protective factor in women that is responsible for the changing pattern of CHD around the time of the female menopause.

FIGURE 1: Age-specific CHD death rates by sex, England and Wales, 1992

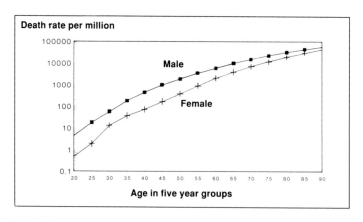

Source: See reference 1.

Social class

Any explanation of CHD risk needs to take into account social class and ethnic variations. As in men, the prevalence of CHD among women shows a strong inverse social class gradient.

Mortality

There is an extremely wide gap in CHD mortality rates between women in manual and non-manual groups.[2] Between 1971 and 1981, the rates of CHD increased among women in manual social classes, and decreased among women in non-manual social classes, leading to a widening social class gap. The trend is similar among men (see Figure 2). The social class gap is much wider in women: in 1981, death rates from CHD among women aged 20-59 in social class V (SMR 161) were nearly four times as high as those among women in social class I (SMR 43); among men aged 20-64, the difference was two-fold.

FIGURE 2: Standardised mortality ratios* for select causes of death in Great Britain, 1970-72 and 1979-83, for manual and non-manual groups

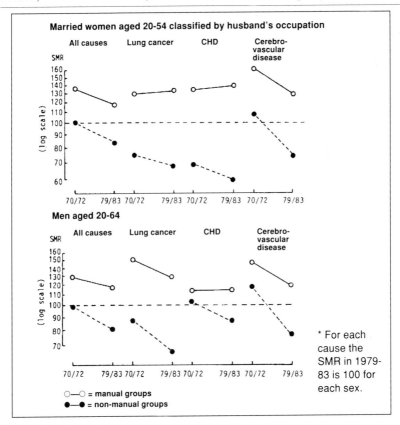

Source: See reference 2.

The strong social class gradient in CHD mortality is also seen among Whitehall male civil servants: men in lower grades have higher rates of CHD mortality than men in higher grades.

Morbidity

The original Whitehall I study – a longitudinal study set up to examine social gradients in CHD mortality among British civil servants – included 18,000 men, but no women. In contrast, the newer Whitehall II study[3] includes 3,413 women and 6,895 men aged 35-55. All participants are classified by their grade of employment, covering social classes I to III. The Whitehall II study has the advantage that women are classified by their own grade of employment.*

The grade differences seen in CHD morbidity in Whitehall II parallel those seen in mortality in Whitehall I. Whitehall II reveals a marked inverse social class gradient in CHD morbidity rates in both sexes: women and men in the lower employment grades have a higher prevalence of angina (measured by the Rose angina questionnaire) and of ischaemia as measured by electro-cardiogram (ECG), than those in higher grades. (See also *Angina in women* on page 67.)

Risk factors for coronary heart disease

The major risk factors for CHD are the same for women as for men, but they operate at a different level. Smoking, high blood cholesterol and hypertension all predict CHD in women but, for any given level, constitute a much smaller risk. Other important risk factors in women include obesity and diabetes. Furthermore, the social class and ethnic differences in CHD rates and risk factors among women also require special attention.

Smoking

Smoking is the most important preventable cause of CHD. The effect of smoking

---

Although women are classified by their husband's occupation, husband's social class predicts mortality better in married women than their own social class. There may be several reasons for this. Firstly, if women are classified by their own social class, a large proportion who are 'unemployed' are missed out. Secondly, there is evidence that married women who also work still do the majority of domestic chores, while married men only do one job. Therefore, a woman's own occupation may not reveal as much about a woman's life as a man's occupation does about his. Thirdly, it may be that on average women marry men in jobs of higher status and higher pay, and that this is a better indicator of the social conditions in which the woman lives than her own. Fourthly, it is interesting that, when women are grouped by a social classification that is not based on occupation – such as housing tenure or car ownership – their rates of CHD show a similar gradient to that for men.

on CHD risk is dose-dependent. Pre-menopausal smokers have three times the risk of heart attack of non-smokers, and women who smoke more than 40 cigarettes a day increase their risk 20-fold. Diabetic women who smoke have a particularly high risk.[4]

In line with other surveys, the Whitehall II study shows a dramatic inverse social class gradient in smoking: the lower the grade, the higher the prevalence of smoking, among both women and men. Smoking is the risk factor that differs most between employment categories. Furthermore, in all but the lowest grade (clerical and office-support category) more women smoke than men.

Cholesterol

It has previously been suggested that total cholesterol does not predict CHD in women. However, although there are fewer studies which include women, an analysis of pooled data from 14 prospective studies which did include women shows that, in terms of relative risk, total cholesterol level predicts CHD in women at least as strongly as in men[5] (see Table 1). Above age 65, total

---

TABLE 1: Predictive power of cholesterol fraction for prospective CHD risk

Total cholesterol
Relative risk of fatal CHD comparing >6.2 mmol/l vs <5.2 mmol/l

	Women	**Men**
< 65 years	2.44*	1.73*
≥ 65 years	1.12*	1.32*

HDL cholesterol
Relative risk of fatal CHD comparing <1.3 mmol/l vs >1.6 mmol/l

	Women	**Men**
< 65 years	2.13*	2.31*
≥ 65 years	1.75*	1.09

LDL cholesterol
Relative risk of fatal CHD comparing >4.1 mmol/l vs < 3.6 mmol/l

	Women	**Men**
< 65 years	3.27*	1.92*
≥ 65 years	1.13	1.51*

---

* relative risk greater than 1.0: $p < 0.05$

Relative risk compares undesirable and desirable levels of cholesterol fraction on the basis of the US National Cholesterol Education Program cut-points. Measurement taken before and after age 65.

Source: See reference 5.

cholesterol levels predict CHD less well, in women as well as men. Overall, then, the relative risk of CHD associated with high cholesterol levels is similar in both women and men, although for any given level of cholesterol, women have a lower absolute risk of CHD.

Table 1 also shows the relative risk of CHD for different levels of HDL cholesterol and LDL cholesterol in women and men. A high level of HDL cholesterol is protective, and for women and men under 65, the relative risk associated with low HDL levels is very similar. Above age 65, however, HDL cholesterol levels appear to be predictive of CHD risk – and still protective – in women, but not in men.

For LDL cholesterol, before age 65, the relative risk of CHD associated with a high LDL cholesterol level appears to be higher in women than in men, but above age 65, the relative risk reduces and is less in women than in men.

The picture which emerges from this analysis of pooled data is that levels of total cholesterol, HDL cholesterol and LDL cholesterol do predict risk of CHD among younger women – as they do among younger men – but the predictive power lessens in both older women and men. Above age 65, low HDL cholesterol continues to predict CHD risk in women, but LDL cholesterol does not seem to be predictive in women.

Among younger adults, total cholesterol levels tend to be higher in men. However, at age 45-50 there is a crossover as cholesterol levels continue to rise in women but even off in men (see Chapter 7). The menopause is associated with changes in lipid levels. The Whitehall II study found that post-menopausal women had higher, less desirable, age-adjusted levels of total cholesterol and LDL cholesterol (assessed by measurement of apolipoprotein B), although 'protective' HDL cholesterol levels (assessed by measurement of apolipoprotein AI) were also slightly higher than those in pre-menopausal women of the same age.[6] It is possible that these differences contribute to the reduced sex difference in CHD mortality rates at older ages.

There are no significant differences in total cholesterol levels between employment grades in Whitehall II: cholesterol levels in all groups are high.

However, cholesterol sub-fractions do show differences between grades of employment. Among women and men, there are significantly higher levels of HDL cholesterol in higher grades, which is consistent with the protective function of HDL cholesterol.

Among women, there is an inverse relationship between levels of LDL cholesterol and grade of employment: women in lower employment grades have higher LDL cholesterol levels. There are no differences in levels of LDL cholesterol by grade of employment in men. The ratio of LDL cholesterol to HDL cholesterol (an index of atherogenic risk) is more favourable in the higher grade women and men than among those in lower grades. Triglyceride levels are inversely related to employment grade among both women and men: lower grades have higher triglyceride levels.

Haemostatic factors

Plasma fibrinogen, another potential explanatory factor for the social class gradient in CHD, shows an inverse gradient by grade of employment, in both women and men in Whitehall II. The lower the grade, the higher the plasma fibrinogen.[6] However, Whitehall II also indicates that sex differences in CHD risk are not directly related to haemostatic factors. Plasma fibrinogen levels are higher in women than in men, in keeping with other studies, and higher among post-menopausal women than pre-menopausal women. Factor VII shows no gradient by employment grade, and no sex difference until after the menopause when Factor VII activity is higher among women.

Blood pressure

The Framingham study found that, after 20 years of follow-up, the relative risk of cardiovascular disease associated with raised systolic blood pressure was similar in women and men aged 45-74, although it has been suggested that hypertension may be a stronger risk factor in women than men.[4] For women, however, the absolute risk of cardiovascular disease is lower for any given blood pressure level.

Blood pressure tends to rise with age in industrialised countries. Average systolic blood pressures are higher in young men than in young women in the UK but, in the 55-64 year age group a crossover occurs and, above this age, average levels are higher in women than men[7, 8] (see Figure 3). The steeper rise in blood pressure with age in women than in men has also been found in

FIGURE 3: Mean systolic blood pressure in women and men, 1991/92, England

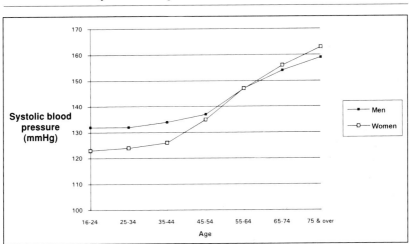

Source: See reference 7.

FIGURE 4: Blood pressure levels among women in different age groups, England, 1991/92

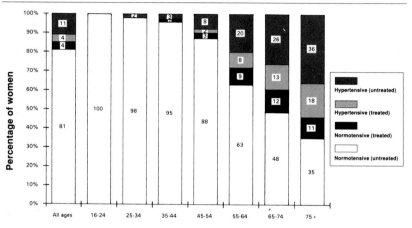

Normotensive = systolic <160mmHg and diastolic <95mmHg
Hypertensive = systolic >160mmHg and diastolic >95mmHg
'Treated' means taking medication for high blood pressure.

Percentages may not add up to 100 due to rounding.

Source: See reference 7.

Whitehall II, and blood pressures in women eventually match male figures. It is possible that a crossover will be seen later.

Although the prevalence of hypertension in under-55 year olds is lower in women than in men, above the age of 64 the reverse is true. Hypertension is common in older women, and with an ageing population this is particularly important. In 1991/92, among women aged 55-64 in England, 37% were hypertensive or being treated for high blood pressure.[7] Among 65-74 year old women this proportion rose to over half (52%) and among women aged 75 and over, the proportion is two-thirds (65%). (See Figure 4).

These results are consistent with a major role for hypertension in the explanation of the age trends in CHD in both sexes.

In the Whitehall II study, there are no employment grade differences in either systolic or diastolic blood pressure among women or men.

Thus, although there are large social class differences in CHD, these are not reflected in total cholesterol or blood pressure levels. These risk factors clearly do not explain the social class differences in coronary disease.

Obesity and central adiposity

Obesity is associated with an increased risk of CHD (see Chapter 8). In Whitehall II, as in the general UK population, body mass index (BMI, or weight/height^2) shows an inverse social class gradient – the lower the employment grade, the higher the BMI – which is stronger in women than in men. Although some of the risk associated with obesity is mediated through raised blood cholesterol and blood pressure, other factors related to obesity may also be related to CHD risk.

The distribution of body fat is now recognised as a contributing factor in the development of CHD, independent of relative body weight. There are links between central adiposity, insulin resistance and raised triglycerides which may relate to cardiovascular risk. The male (or android) pattern of obesity, with a high waist to hip ratio, is associated with higher risk of CHD than the female (gynoid) pattern of lower waist to hip ratio, which may partly explain the sex differences in CHD. The Gothenburg study in Sweden,[9] for example, found that differences in blood pressure, smoking, blood cholesterol and body mass index only explained a small part of the sex difference in CHD rates, but when waist:hip ratio was also considered, the sex difference in CHD risk almost disappeared. Body fat distribution, or factors closely related to it, may thus be part of the explanation for sex differences in CHD.

Furthermore, the higher average waist to hip ratio among women in manual groups,[7] as well as their higher BMI, may help explain their higher CHD rates.

Ethnic variations

There are marked ethnic differences in the rates of CHD in the UK. Adults born in the Indian sub-continent, but living in England and Wales, have a higher risk of CHD than adults born in the UK and the excess is greater among women. Women born in the Indian sub-continent but living in England and Wales, have a CHD death rate that is about 50% greater than other women living in England and Wales. This excess (Standardised Mortality Ratio 146) is greater among Indian women than among Indian men (SMR 136). Among Afro-Caribbean adults, on the other hand, the risk of CHD is smaller. Afro-Caribbean women (SMR 76) have about three-quarters the CHD rates of women from England and Wales, but are rather less well protected than Afro-Caribbean men (SMR 45).[10]

Within the civil service, there is a large grade difference in ethnicity, and most non-Caucasians are in the lower grades. Smoking rates are low both among Afro-Caribbean women and men, and among men from the Indian sub-continent, even when adjustments are made for grade differences. Women from the Indian sub-continent tend not to smoke. Thus smoking behaviour does not explain the high prevalence and mortality from CHD among women from the Indian

FIGURE 5: Standardised Mortality Ratios for CHD among women aged 20-69, by country of birth, England and Wales, 1979-83

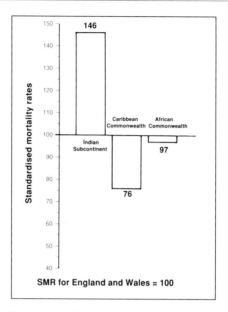

Source: See reference 10.

sub-continent. Research suggests that it is related to the metabolic syndrome of insulin resistance.

The insulin resistance syndrome, associated with a striking tendency to central obesity in South Asian women and men, is the most plausible explanation for their high CHD mortality.[11] South Asian women in the UK show a pronounced tendency to central obesity, evident in a higher waist:hip ratio, and correlations with insulin and triglyceride levels are stronger with waist:hip ratio than for body mass index. Control of obesity and increased physical activity may be particularly important for the prevention of CHD in South Asian women.

Diabetes

Diabetes increases the risk of CHD, in both women and men. However, diabetes imposes a greater risk of CHD in women than in men,[12] and so among diabetics the sex difference in CHD risk is reduced. Among non-diabetics, the relative risk of CHD is between three and five times higher among men than women. However, female diabetics have the same risk of CHD as the average for all men. Thus, for a woman, being diabetic means losing protection from CHD.

It is becoming clear that the metabolic disturbances associated with non-insulin dependent diabetes are important in CHD risk. It is possible that a high waist:hip ratio (the 'male' pattern of obesity) increases the likelihood of diabetes and also of CHD. Women with a higher waist:hip ratio have increased risk of impaired glucose tolerance and adult onset diabetes. This could help explain the partial loss of protection in women who are diabetic.

Family history

Women with a family history of CHD have a greater risk of CHD than those without. Furthermore, women whose parents died from CHD at a younger age have a higher relative risk of dying from the disease both compared to those whose parents developed CHD at an older age, and compared to those whose parents who did not have CHD.[13] Figure 6 shows the relative risks among women aged 30-55 of non-fatal myocardial infarction, fatal CHD and angina, in groups with different family histories.

FIGURE 6: Relative risk of CHD events among women aged 30-55

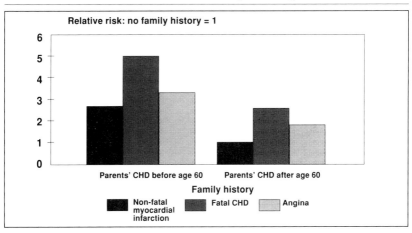

Source: See reference 13.

Angina in women

There are also sex differences in the spectrum of clinical presentation. While myocardial infarction (heart attack) rates are much greater in men than in women, sex differences in classical angina are much less marked. In Whitehall II, among 35-55 year olds, angina (measured by the Rose angina questionnaire) was more common among women than men.[3] In the Framingham study, the incidence of angina in women and men aged 55-64 was similar, with a male to female ratio of approximately 1.3:1 – considerably less than the sex ratio for myocardial infarction.

However, there is a debate about whether there is a different pathogenesis for angina in women. It seems that women with a typical history of classical angina may have either atherosclerotic CHD or may have ischaemia (inadequate blood supply to the heart muscle) of some other pathogenesis, which might, for example, be related to spasm of the coronary arteries or be of some other origin. It has been suggested that there may be a reporting bias (ie women may be relatively more likely to report angina), but this does not seem to be the case.

Although women have a higher prevalence of angina than men, they have a lower prevalence of ischaemia when measured by electrocardiogram (ECG). In Whitehall II, among men who had angina, 17.6% also had ECG abnormalities, indicating possible or probable ischaemia, compared with only 5.8% of men who did not have angina. These are similar to the percentages reported in other studies. Among women, however, there was no significant difference in prevalence of ECG abnormalities between those with angina and those without: 9.7% of women who reported angina also had abnormal ECGs, compared to 6.8% of those who did not report angina. Thus women have a higher prevalence of angina than men, but a lower prevalence of ischaemic ECGs. The same phenomenon was reported in the Framingham study.[14]

Furthermore, coronary angiography (see page 31) reveals that women with angina are less likely to have atheroma in the coronary vessels than men with angina. In the Coronary Artery Surgery Study,[15] for example, coronary angiography among women and men with a typical history of angina revealed that only 72% of women had severe narrowing of the coronary vessels (more than 70% stenosis) compared with 93% of men.

While angina predicts mortality in both women and men, the prognosis of angina is worse in men than in women. In the Framingham study, one in four men with angina had a coronary attack within five years; the risk among women was about half this.[16] However, the survival advantage for women is lost once myocardial infarction develops: case fatality rates are similar in both sexes. Data from Framingham, for example, show that survival rates, or absolute mortality risks, after non-fatal heart attacks are similar in women and men. In both sexes, 39% died within a decade.[16] However, because women seem to be diagnosed and treated later in the course of their illness than men, it is difficult to compare case fatality rates between women and men (see Chapter 4).

Thus, there may be a different spectrum of clinical presentation in women and men. Women with angina may have normal coronary arteries more often than men, but they are nevertheless also at risk of the serious manifestations of CHD.[17]

Conclusion

Understanding of CHD risk comes largely from studies among men. The Whitehall II study includes over 3,000 female civil servants, classified by grade of employment, and provides the opportunity to examine CHD risk and risk factors in women as well as men.

The major risk factors for CHD are the same in both sexes. Smoking, high blood cholesterol and hypertension all predict CHD in women, but for any given level they constitute a much smaller risk than in men. Diabetes is a particularly important risk factor in women, and imposes a greater risk of CHD than in men. Obesity is also associated with an increased risk of CHD, and sex differences in body fat distribution may partly explain the differences in CHD risk.

Among women, as among men, there are large social class and ethnic differences in CHD rates. Women in manual social classes have higher rates than those in non-manual groups: the gap is wider than among men. South Asian women have particularly high rates of CHD. The social and ethnic variations in risk factors, morbidity and mortality need to be taken into account in understanding and addressing CHD risk.

This section is based on a paper prepared for the National Forum for Coronary Heart Disease Prevention by Professor M G Marmot and Dr E J Brunner, both of the Department of Epidemiology and Public Health, University College London. Professor Marmot is an individual member of the Forum.

References

1   Office of Population Censuses and Surveys. 1993. *Mortality statistics: Cause. England and Wales 1992.* DH2 Series, no 19. London: HMSO.
2   Marmot MG, McDowall ME. 1986. Mortality decline and widening social inequalities. *Lancet*; i: 274-276.
3   Marmot MG, Davey Smith G, Stansfeld S, Patel C, North F, Head J, White I, Brunner EJ, Feeney A. 1991. Health inequalities among British civil servants: the Whitehall II Study. *Lancet*; 337: 1387-1393.
4   Jackson G. 1994. Coronary artery disease and women. *British Medical Journal*; 309: 555-556.
5   Manolio TA, Pearson TA, Wenger NK, Barrett-Connor E, Payne GH, Harlan WR. 1992. Cholesterol and heart disease in older persons and women: review of an NHLBI workshop (June 1990). *Annals of Epidemiology*; 2: 161-176.

6   Brunner EJ, Marmot MG, White IR, O'Brien JR, Etherington MD, Slavin BM, Kearney EM, Davey Smith G. 1993. Gender and employment grade differences in blood cholesterol, apolipoproteins and haemostatic factors in the Whitehall II study. *Atherosclerosis*; 102: 195-207.

7   Breeze E, Maidment A, Bennett N, Flatley J, Carey S. 1994. *Health survey for England 1992. A survey carried out by the Social Survey Division of OPCS on behalf of the Department of Health.* London: HMSO.

8   Gregory J, Foster K, Tyler H, Wiseman M. Social Survey Division, OPCS.1990. *The dietary and nutritional survey of British adults.* London: HMSO.

9   Larsson B, Bengtsson C, Bjorntorp P, Lapidus L, Sjostrom L et al. 1992. Is abdominal body fat distribution a major explanation for the sex difference in the incidence of myocardial infarction? *American Journal of Epidemiology*; 135: 266-273.

10   Balarajan R. 1991. Ethnic differences in mortality from ischaemic heart disease and cerebrovascular disease in England and Wales. *British Medical Journal*; 302: 560-564.

11   McKeigue PM, Shah B, Marmot M. 1991. Relation of central obesity and insulin resistance with high diabetes prevalence and cardiovascular risk in South Asians. *Lancet*; 337: 382-386.

12   Barrett-Connor EL, Cohn BA, Wingard DL, Edelstein SL. 1991. Why is diabetes mellitus a stronger risk factor for fatal ischaemic heart disease in women than in men? *Journal of the American Medical Association*; 265: 627-631.

13   Colditz GA, Stampfer MJ, Willett WC, Rosner B, Speizer FE, Hennekens CH. 1986. A prospective study of parental history of myocardial infarction and coronary heart disease in women. *American Journal of Epidemiology*; 123: 48-58.

14   Waldron I. 1983. Sex differences in illness incidence, prognosis and mortality: issues and evidence. *Social Science and Medicine*; 17: 1107-1123.

15   Chaitman BR, Bourassa MG, Davis K, Rogers WJ, Tyras DH, Berger R, Kennedy JW, Fisher L, Judkins MP, Mock MB, Killip T. 1981. Angiographic prevalence of high-risk coronary artery disease in patient subsets (CASS). *Circulation*; 64: 360-367.

16   Kannel WB, Abbott RD. 1987. Incidence and prognosis of myocardial infarction in women: the Framingham study. In: Eaker ED, Packard B, Wenger NK (eds). *Coronary heart disease in women* (p208-214). New York: Haymarket Doyma.

17   Kannel WB, Sorlie P, McNamara PM. 1979. Prognosis after initial myocardial infarction: the Framingham study. *American Journal of Cardiology*; 44: 53-59.

CHAPTER 6

Smoking

Smoking patterns among girls and women. Why do they smoke?

AMANDA AMOS

SUMMARY

Smoking kills over 31,000 women in the UK each year. The main smoking-related disease is coronary heart disease. Smoking is the single most preventable cause of ill health among women.

Cigarette smoking has declined among adults in the UK but the decline has been slower among women than men, and the gap between women's and men's cigarette smoking rates has virtually disappeared. The rate of decline in smoking depends on the cessation rate (women are less likely to quit smoking than men), and on the uptake rate (smoking is now more common among girls than boys). Cigarette smoking is increasingly associated with social disadvantage in both sexes.

Factors influencing smoking patterns among girls and women include: personal factors (perceived benefits of smoking, lack of self-esteem); social factors (whether family members or friends smoke); and environmental and community factors including tobacco promotion and price and availability of cigarettes.

The majority of women smokers want to give up. Women from manual social classes are less likely to give up successfully: many use cigarettes as a coping strategy. Women also use cigarettes as a means of controlling moods and unwanted feelings. These factors need to be addressed when planning any cessation programme.

The UK has one of the highest levels of smoking-related disease in the world. In 1988, smoking killed an estimated 31,620 women in the UK.[1] Of these, 8,536 died from coronary heart disease (CHD), the main smoking-related cause of death among women. Smoking is now recognised as the single most important preventable cause of ill health among women.

However, since women took up smoking later than men, it is only in the past 10 years that the full impact of this habit has begun to be fully appreciated. Concern has focused on two main issues: the true extent of the health risks of smoking to women, and the changing patterns of cigarette smoking among girls and women.

The social distribution of cigarette smoking has undergone marked changes over the past few decades in the UK, and three important trends have emerged:
1   Although smoking has declined among adults, the gap between cigarette smoking rates among women and men has virtually disappeared.
2   Cigarette smoking is now more common among girls than boys.
3   Cigarette smoking among both women and men has become increasingly associated with social disadvantage.

Adults

Although cigarette smoking has declined among both women and men over the last 20 years, there has been increasing concern about the changing pattern, particularly among women. Although the habit used to be much more common among men, the gap between women and men has now narrowed, and by 1992, when 29% of men and 28% of women were cigarette smokers, it had virtually disappeared.

Cigarette smoking first became widespread among men around the turn of the century. However, it was not until the 1920s and 30s that it became socially acceptable for women to be seen smoking in public and the habit began to spread. By the 1950s and 60s cigarette smoking had reached its peak and some 40% of British women were smokers. Since the mid-70s, the prevalence of cigarette smoking has fallen: by 1992, 28% of British women were smoking cigarettes.[2]

However, the decline in smoking rates has been much slower among women than men (see Figure 1). Between 1972 and 1992, cigarette smoking among women declined from 41% to 28% – a fall of 32% or 13 percentage points. During the same period men's smoking rates fell from 52% to 29% – a fall of 44% or 23 percentage points. Thus the difference in smoking prevalence between women and men has been narrowing over time, and by 1992 it had virtually disappeared. In Scotland the rates of smoking among women are now the same as those among men.

FIGURE 1: Cigarette smoking prevalence among adults aged 16 and over, by sex, 1948-92, Great Britain

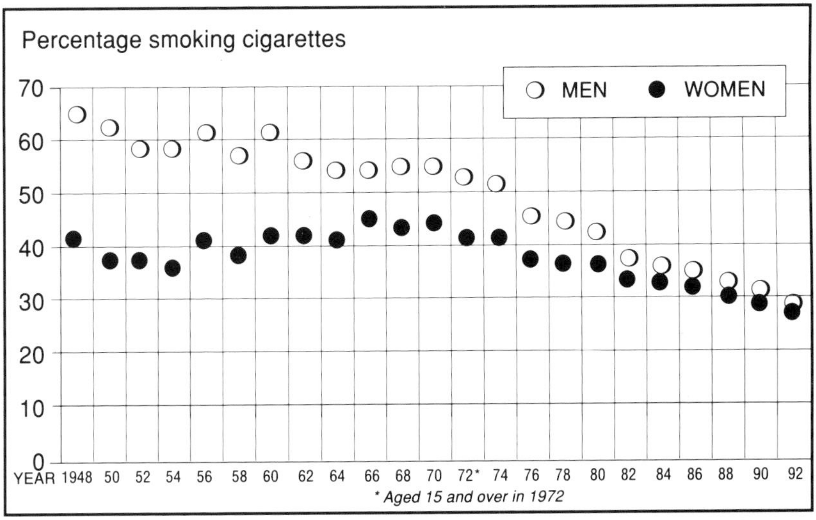

Percentage smoking cigarettes

○ MEN   ● WOMEN

YEAR: 1948 50 52 54 56 58 60 62 64 66 68 70 72* 74 76 78 80 82 84 86 88 90 92
* Aged 15 and over in 1972

Source: See references 3 (1948-70), and 2 (1972-92).

However, although the rate of decline in smoking in the UK has been greater than in most other countries, over the past few years it has begun to slow down among both women and men. Between 1972 and 1982 the prevalence of smoking among women declined on average by 0.8% a year. Between 1982 and 1992 this fell to 0.5% per year.

Factors influencing the rate of decline in smoking

The rate of decline in smoking is dependent on two factors: the *cessation rate* and the *uptake rate*.

Cessation rate

Women have lower 'quitting' rates of smoking cigarettes than men. In 1992, 44% of women who had ever smoked said that they had quit compared to 52% of men.[2] However, much of the apparent sex difference in cessation rates can be explained by a significant proportion of men replacing cigarettes with other types of tobacco, such as pipes or cigars. Thus, while the rate of quitting cigarette smoking is much lower in women, the rate of quitting all tobacco smoking is more similar, although it is still slightly lower among women than among men.[4]

Since 1972, cessation rates in both women and men have slowed down. For women, the cessation rate fell from 1.3% of smokers quitting every year between 1972 and 1982, to 1.1% between 1982 and 1992.[2]

Uptake rate

A more important reason for the narrowing gap in smoking rates has been the slower decline in rates of starting to smoke among girls and young women compared to boys and young men.

School children

The traditional pattern of higher rates of cigarette smoking among teenage boys than girls has now reversed, and cigarette smoking, both regular and occasional, is now more common among 11-15 year old girls than boys.[5] There has been only a small decrease in smoking rates between 1982 and 1992 for both girls and boys.

Older teenagers

By 1990, cigarette smoking rates were also higher among young women aged 16-19 and 20-24 than among young men of the same age. For example, 32% of women aged 16-19 were smokers compared to 28% of men in this age group. The higher smoking rates among young women were not unexpected, and follow trends among younger girls and boys. Although the positions had reversed in 1992, there is no obvious explanation for this: the fluctuations may be due to chance variation in the samples.

FIGURE 2: Percentage of secondary school children aged 11-15 smoking cigarettes either regularly or occasionally, 1982-92, England

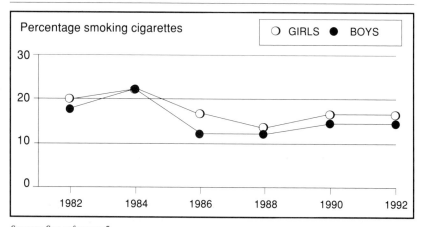

Source: See reference 5.

The decline in smoking rates between 1972 and 1992 was more rapid in young men than young women. This is due both to a slower decline in the uptake rate and to slightly lower cessation rates among women (see *Cessation rate* on page 73).

Social disadvantage

Another cause for concern is the increasing link between cigarette smoking and social disadvantage. Among both women and men, cigarette smoking is now associated with several indicators of social disadvantage, including socioeconomic group, educational level and income.[6,7]

This pattern is relatively recent. In the late 1960s, some 40% of women smoked cigarettes, and the rate was similar across all income groups. By 1992, however, the picture had changed considerably, with a strong inverse social class gradient (see Table 1). Only 13% of women living in 'professional' households smoked, compared to 35% of those living in 'unskilled manual' households. This social class difference is due to both smoking uptake and cessation rates: working class women are more likely to start smoking, and less likely to quit.

TABLE 1: Cigarette smoking prevalence among women aged 16 or over by economic group, 1992, Great Britain

	Current smoker	Ex-regular smoker	Never smoked
	%	%	%
Professional	13	21	65
Employers and managers	21	26	53
Intermediate and junior non-manual	27	20	53
Skilled manual	31	20	49
Semi-skilled manual	35	18	47
Unskilled manual	35	20	44
All	28	21	52

Source: See reference 2.

Among women from non-manual households, 49% who had ever smoked have quit, compared to only 37% of smokers from manual households.

Thus, although smoking has declined in the UK, the rate of decline has been slower in women than in men. This is due to a combination of slower quitting rates and a slower decline in starting to smoke. Smoking has also become increasingly associated with social disadvantage.

Factors that influence smoking among young girls and women

Similar trends in women's cigarette smoking have been seen in those countries which have the longest history of smoking, suggesting that similar forces may have been operating. Research from several countries, primarily the United States and the UK, has shown that there is no single reason which explains the changing smoking patterns among women, or why young girls are still taking up the habit. However, several important factors have been identified, and although the picture is not complete, this information will help develop more effective strategies to reduce smoking among women. These factors fall into three categories: individual and personal, social, and environmental and community.[8,9,10,11] Although they apply to both sexes, their relative importance for each may be different.

Individual and personal factors

Knowledge, attitudes and beliefs about smoking are important in determining whether a girl starts to smoke. The perceived costs and benefits include not only health consequences, but also the perception of 'What will smoking do for me?'

Positive or negative attitudes towards smoking consistently predict smoking onset. This may be more important for girls than boys. One study, for example, found that girls who thought that smoking 'made people look more grown up', 'helped to calm nerves', 'control weight' and 'give confidence' were the most likely to start smoking.[12]

Smoking is often perceived as a way of dealing with uncomfortable changes in the moods and feelings of adolescence. It may be seen as creating a positive adult self-image, giving teenagers something to do with their hands or providing a nicotine buzz. Once they have started smoking, girls seem to be more dependent than boys at any given level of smoking, and find it more difficult to give up.

Girls who start smoking are also more likely to have lower self-esteem, be under-achievers at school, be alienated from school, and have lower academic goals.

Social factors

Girls are more likely to start smoking if family members smoke, particularly older brothers or sisters. There is evidence to suggest that family smoking patterns may be a more important influence for girls than boys.[13]

A friend or a best friend who smokes is also an important factor. This may be due to peer pressure, or simply the influence of having friends who share similar views and attitudes. For example, girls who are more socially precocious (ie have a boyfriend, go to discos or go out socially), are more likely to smoke.

This may explain why girls have higher smoking rates than boys in their early teens, as girls start to associate with older boys.

School also has an influence both in terms of the health education that is provided, and whether there is a school policy on smoking.

Girls' smoking rates are also influenced by available spending money.

Environmental and community factors

Social attitudes and norms are one of the most important influences on the changing pattern of smoking. During the past century, smoking by girls and women has become far more socially acceptable, even in the face of increased public disapproval for smoking generally over the past few years.

Religious and cultural factors are important. Some religions do not permit women to smoke: Asian girls in the UK, for example, have much lower smoking rates than girls from other ethnic backgrounds.

However, the most important environmental influences on smoking among girls are tobacco promotion and price and availability of cigarettes.

Tobacco promotion

The tobacco industry consistently argues that tobacco promotion does not encourage smoking but simply affects brand choice among adults. A considerable body of evidence now shows that children from an early age are aware of and understand tobacco advertisements, that tobacco advertising both influences uptake of smoking and reinforces smoking among young people, and that tobacco sponsorship acts as advertising.[14] Furthermore, countries which have banned tobacco advertising have witnessed a faster decline in cigarette smoking among young people than countries which have not.[15]

It is estimated that about £100 million is spent on advertising and promoting tobacco products each year in the UK.[16] Young women have been clearly identified as a key target group by the tobacco industry, and a variety of strategies are used to reach them.[17] Some of the most important include:

1 Promoting images designed specifically to appeal to women through advertising and sponsorship
2 Producing new brands or versions of brands which are particularly appealing for women, for example low tar, longer length cigarettes
3 Using women's magazines to reach women.

Although the voluntary agreement between the industry and government is intended to protect young women from tobacco advertising, it is clearly failing. For example, millions of young women are exposed to such advertisements in women's magazines.[18] The sum spent on tobacco advertising in women's magazines has increased in real terms over the last few years.

Furthermore, in addition to paid advertising, positive media images of women smoking in films, television and fashion photographs reinforce the advertising images. For example, a 1991 survey of fashion and style magazines aimed at young people found that many carried positive images of smoking in their editorial sections.[19]

Price and availability of cigarettes
Price and availability of cigarettes influence whether young people start smoking. For every 1% increase in the real price of cigarettes, there is an estimated 1.4% decline in tobacco consumption among young people.[20] Furthermore, the more easily available cigarettes are, the more likely children are to buy them. Despite the law which prohibits the sale of cigarettes to children under the age of 16, over £100 million is spent by children under 16 buying cigarettes each year.[21]

Cessation

There is considerable debate, but surprisingly little research, on whether women find it more difficult than men to give up smoking. Although cigarette smoking cessation rates are lower among women than men, it is uncertain whether women make more attempts to quit before they finally succeed. However, at every level of consumption, women are more likely than men to think that they would find it difficult to give up for a day.[2] Evidence also suggests that the factors which influence whether an attempt is successful may be different for women and men.

Social disadvantage seems to be important in determining whether or not women are successful in giving up smoking. Women from manual socioeconomic groups are not only more likely to smoke than those from non-manual groups but they are also less likely to successfully give up smoking.

Research examining the associations between smoking, low income and caring for children has indicated that, for many women, smoking is one of the few ways of coping with the difficult circumstances in which they live.[22,23] In a life of relative poverty, cigarettes can be perceived as a necessity, and a luxury which symbolises participation in the lifestyle of the wider society. Buying cigarettes was often the only spending the women did for themselves. Smoking a cigarette provided a break from caring, where mothers were able to rest and refuel. It became a way of breaking up the day, and was an important way of creating a space between a mother and her children when the demands became too much.

Similarly, a study in Southampton also concluded that many women on lower incomes use smoking as a coping strategy and as a means of dealing with the stress in their lives, although this was not true for all the women smokers in the study.[24] There is a need for more research to explore these issues.

Several other studies have suggested that adult women, like teenage girls, use cigarettes as a means of dealing with unwanted feelings and controlling moods, more so than do men. At least one in four women claim that they smoke in order to control their mood.[25]

The majority of women want to give up smoking.[2] However, women are unlikely to achieve their aim unless the positive attitudes and beliefs about the benefits of giving up smoking outweigh the perceived negative consequences such as gaining weight, unless they are confident about their ability to give up, and unless they live in an environment which supports them giving up and maintaining a non-smoking status.

This section is based on a paper prepared for the National Forum for Coronary Heart Disease Prevention by Dr Amanda Amos, Senior Lecturer in Health Promotion at the University of Edinburgh.

References

1   Health Education Authority. 1991. *The smoking epidemic*. London: Health Education Authority.
2   Office of Population Censuses and Surveys. 1994. *General household survey, 1992*. London: HMSO.
3   Tobacco Advisory Council smoking statistics cited in: Wald N, Nicholaides-Bouman A (eds). 1988. *UK smoking statistics*. Oxford: Oxford University Press.
4   Office of Population Censuses and Surveys. 1992. *General household survey, 1990*. London: HMSO.
5   Thomas M, Holroyd S, Goddard E. OPCS. 1993. *Smoking among secondary school children in 1992*. London: HMSO.
6   Marsh A, McKay S. 1994. *Poor smokers*. London: Policy Studies Institute.
7   ASH Working Group on Women and Smoking. 1993. *Her share of misfortune*. London: Action on Smoking and Health.
8   UICC. 1990. *A manual on tobacco and young people for the industrialised world*. Geneva: UICC.
9   ASH Working Group on Women and Smoking. 1989. *Teenage girls and smoking*. London: Action on Smoking and Health.
10 Bellew B, Wayne D. 1991. Prevention of smoking among schoolchildren: review of research and recommended actions. *Health Education Journal*; 50: 3-8.
11 Chollat-Traquet C. 1992. *Women and tobacco*. Geneva: World Health Organization.
12 Charlton A, Blair V. 1989. Predicting the onset of smoking in boys and girls. *Social Science and Medicine*; 29: 813-818.
13 Goddard E. 1990. *Why children start smoking*. London: HMSO.
14 Hastings GB, Aitken PP, MacKintosh AM. 1991. *From the billboard to the playground*. London: Cancer Research Campaign.
15 New Zealand Toxic Substances Board. 1989. *Health or tobacco: an end to tobacco advertising and promotion*. Wellington: Department of Health.
16 Action on Smoking and Health. 1993. *Tobacco advertising – the case for a ban*. 4th edition. London: ASH.

17   Amos A. 1990. How women are targeted by the tobacco industry. *World Health Forum*; 11: 416-422.

18   Amos A, Jacobson B, White P. 1991. Cigarette advertising policy and coverage of smoking and health in British women's magazines. *Lancet*; 337: 93-96.

19   Amos A. 1992. *Style and image: tobacco and alcohol images in selected fashion and style magazines in 1991*. London: Health Education Authority.

20   Townsend J. 1988. *Tobacco price and the smoking epidemic*. Smoke-Free Europe 9. Copenhagen: WHO.

21   Derived from House of Commons. 1994. House of Commons Hansard column 666w, 1 March, and House of Commons Hansard column 97, 8 March.

22   Graham H. 1987. Women's smoking and family health. *Social Science and Medicine*; 25: 47-56.

23   Graham H. 1993. *When life's a drag: women, smoking and disadvantage*. London: HMSO.

24   Wells J, Batten L. 1990. Women smoking and coping: an analysis of women's experience of stress. *Health Education Journal*; 49: 57-60.

25   Marsh A, Matheson J. 1983. *Smoking attitudes and behaviour*. London: HMSO.

Policy implications of women and smoking. Is there a special case for action?

BOBBIE JACOBSON

SUMMARY

Policy on smoking must be considered at international, national and local level. Policies to reduce smoking rates among women have an impact not only on coronary heart disease, but also on other smoking-related diseases such as cancer and bronchitis.

Four issues must be addressed: the failure to reduce smoking prevalence among girls and young women; gender differences in the motivation to smoke and the barriers to quitting; the health consequences of smoking among women; and the strong relationship between cigarette smoking and social disadvantage.

Objectives for reducing smoking among women might include: a reduction in the social class gap in cigarette smoking among women; a reduction in the proportion of school age girls who become regular smokers; and achieving a cessation rate for women at least equal to that of men in all age groups. The current national health strategies do not address social class differences or the slower decline in smoking rates among women.

Policy on non-tobacco issues are needed and should include: general education measures, such as improved educational opportunities for women; and social policy measures such as better childcare (health education would have more impact if supported by social policies). Tobacco-centric policies are also needed: a ban on tobacco advertising (women are targeted particularly through women's magazines); pricing policy (women are more price-sensitive than men); smoking education and information; cessation advice; and provision of smoke-free workplaces. Further research is needed on factors affecting smoking uptake, maintenance and cessation among women. In policy terms it is important to look at the woman behind the smoker.

Policy needs to be considered, and addressed, from both the population and the individual point of view. The two are interdependent: policy in the European Union and at national level, for example, will have repercussions on local change.

While it is well recognised that many diseases are multi-causal, it is also worth bearing in mind that many causes are multi-diseasal. Any policies directed at reducing smoking rates will have an impact not only on coronary heart disease (CHD), but also, for example, on cancer rates.

There are four main issues specific to women's smoking patterns and the health consequences, that require an appropriate policy response.

1 The failure to reduce smoking prevalence among teenage girls and young women
2 Gender differences in the motivation to smoke and the barriers to quitting
3 Gender-specific health consequences of smoking
4 The strong relationship between cigarette smoking and social disadvantage.

Smoking has several gender-specific health consequences, with risks for women beyond the three major causes of tobacco-related death, namely CHD, lung cancer and bronchitis. For example, there is a multiplicative effect between cigarette smoking and the oral contraceptive pill: the overall risk of cardiovascular disease increases 10-fold in women who smoke and take the oral contraceptive pill. This is, therefore, an area of public health that specifically affects women, with important policy implications for health professionals and family planning clinics. Family planning could be an important entry point in policy terms.

A strategy needs to include objectives, development of policy, and plans for its implementation.

Objectives

Objectives for reducing smoking among women by the year 2000 might include:

1 A reduction in the social class gap in cigarette smoking between women from non-manual and manual households by 5%
2 A reduction in the percentage of school age girls who become regular smokers by 10%
3 A cessation rate for women at least equal to that of men in all age categories.

The national health strategies for England, Wales, Scotland and Northern Ireland all include targets for reducing the prevalence of cigarette smoking. However, the targets do not address the social class differences in smoking rates, nor the slower decline in smoking rates among women.

Development and implementation of policy

In order to achieve the above objectives there is a need for:

1 a policy on non-tobacco issues such as general education measures and social policy measures, and

2 a tobacco-centric policy on issues specifically relating to smoking such as: a ban on tobacco advertising and promotion, taxation, smoking education and information, cessation advice, provision of a smoke-free norm at work and in public places, and research.

A tobacco-centric policy on its own is an insufficient response to the problem: a far broader approach is needed.

Within a tobacco-centric policy, many of the policy options have been well rehearsed by a wide range of expert groups, although the options have not necessarily been implemented. Any policy approach needs to address both populations and individuals. One of the main problems in the UK is the lack of adequate research to support the policy options.

TABLE 1: What should a policy cover?

A policy aimed at reducing the harmful effects of smoking on women's health should include:

General education measures including:
- improving educational attainment
- community and adult education
- workplace education.

Social policy measures including measures to reduce women's experience of social disadvantage and to better equip them to make healthy choices, for example:
- childcare provision
- parental leave
- flexible working hours
- child benefit
- income support.

Tobacco-centric policy, including:
- a ban on tobacco advertising and promotion
- pricing policy
- smoking education and information
- cessation advice
- provision of a smoke-free norm at work and in public places
- research.

General education

An improvement of opportunities for good educational attainment for all would have an impact on many aspects of health. Community and adult education and workplace education are used particularly by women who have never had any opportunity for higher education.

Social policy

Many changes in social policy would have an impact on the health of women. Although it is clear that, for example, increasing child benefit would not result in an immediate reduction in smoking rates or a decrease in the social class divide, evidence suggests that it would support women's health decisions. Health education would have more impact if supported by other social policies.

Improvements in provision for childcare and parental leave would also have an impact on women's rates of smoking. The UK has among the worst provision in the European Union. Research by Graham,[1] for example, shows that economically disadvantaged women view cigarettes as a luxury, and a means of 'escaping' the difficulties of childcare. Increased support for mothers is likely to improve their chances of quitting.

Tobacco-centric policy

Tobacco-centric policy has the most direct influence on women's smoking rates, and it is in this area that most progress has been made, both in the UK, and increasingly in the European Union.

A ban on tobacco advertising and promotion

A ban on all advertising and promotion of tobacco could have an important impact on smoking rates among girls and women. Norwegian data collected since the introduction of the 1975 Tobacco Act, which covers tobacco advertising and promotion, and education and information, show that there have been very significant falls in smoking rates among teenage girls as well as boys. Norway is one of the few developed countries in which the smoking rates among girls are lower than those among boys.

A ban on the advertising and promotion of tobacco could have a major impact on women smokers. The women's market has been seen as potentially more expandable than the men's market. However, within the UK, at age 15, girls are now more likely to be regular smokers than boys.

The tobacco industry often directs its products at specific groups, including women. This 'segmentation of the market' involves designing and directing a product or brand at a particular part of the market, using a strategy which includes the product, the message, and the medium.

Women are deliberately targeted by tobacco companies in their advertising, particularly for long, slim, lower tar cigarettes. Certain cigarette brands may acquire a female label or image. 'Virginia Slims', for example, a cigarette brand aimed specifically at women, is now America's 15th best selling brand. The image created by the industry for a new brand 'Dakota', in the United States, deliberately tied it to young, socially disadvantaged women. In advertising in black women's magazines, black models are used.

The tobacco companies have also been very successful in aiming low tar cigarettes at women. The low tar market is largely a female market, although the industry is careful not to over-feminise the product.

Young women are influenced by the image of smoking at a very impressionable age. A ban on advertising and promotion of tobacco would protect girls from such messages.

Women's magazines have a major role in educating young women and women across the age groups, about health and health choices, but many still take cigarette advertising.[2] A ban on advertising and promotion would make such health messages for women much clearer.

Pricing policy

Increasing the real price of cigarettes is an effective means of control. There is a very close relationship between changes in the real price of cigarettes and changes in consumption (see Figure 1). Towards the end of the 1980s, the real price of cigarettes fell, and per capita consumption appeared to be rising.

FIGURE 1: The relationship between the price of cigarettes and consumption, 1971-90

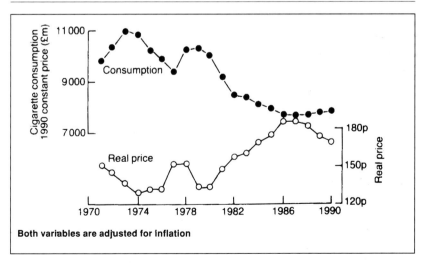

Both variables are adjusted for inflation

Source: See reference 3.

The importance to women of this area of policy is indisputable. Townsend has shown that women are more price sensitive than men.[4] This is likely to be important because, on average, women earn 70% of the earnings of men.

Children are also more price sensitive than adults. In Finland, the 1977 Tobacco Act did not take taxation policy into account sufficiently and, as a result, consumption among both girls and boys has risen, after an initial fall. The future trend is unclear. Disposable pocket money among Finnish children has also increased, which may have an impact on tobacco purchases. In Norway, by contrast, the real price of cigarettes was substantially increased following the introduction of the Tobacco Act in 1975.

Smoking education and information
Labelling of tobacco products has recently been considerably strengthened with the introduction of new regulations on health warnings throughout the European Union. Although the message 'Smoking when pregnant harms your baby' is included in the list of health warnings used in the UK, there is potential to introduce more women-specific health warnings.

Local health care information on the health risks of smoking, specifically for women, could be introduced by health authorities, as part of their local quality strategies for contracting.

There is a wide range of possible policy options for education aimed at reducing women's smoking rates (see Table 2).

TABLE 2: Possible policy options for education aimed at reducing women's smoking rates

SCHOOLS	MASS MEDIA	HEALTH PROMOTION
A gender-specific approach	Non-smoking role models	Confident, female role models in health education
Address girls' concerns about weight	Women's media: information on benefits of giving up smoking, and no tobacco advertising	Cessation advice in the context of women's lives
Integrated approaches including building self-esteem, confidence and skills	Regulation of sponsorship	Avoid victim-blaming
Target girls separately from boys	Information on passive smoking	

Research suggests that girls and women have different preoccupations with cigarettes to those held by boys and men.[5] A more gender-specific approach in education may be appropriate, and particularly a strategy that targets girls separately from boys in schools.

There is a need for very positive female role models in health education. The Health Education Authority's 'Nic O'Teen' campaign provides a good example of the need for gender-specific models. Although it was an extremely popular campaign directed at school children, the Superman image appealed far more to boys than to girls.

Unfortunately, very few well-known positive female role models have been used so far. A poster promoting physical activity, for example, used the somewhat unknown swimmer June Croft. Many popular female role models, such as Madonna, on the other hand, are often seen smoking.

Cessation advice

Smoking cessation advice for women will be most effective if it is considered in the context of women's lives and if it extends beyond individual cessation programmes based in primary care.

Cessation courses could be effectively directed at predominantly female workplaces. However, if it is mainly women in secretarial and clerical grades who smoke, it is important not to direct courses at executive directors. Using existing women's groups, providing female-led courses, linking cessation advice with stress counselling, recruiting women through well-women and family planning clinics or gynaecology departments, may all be effective. However, the different approaches need to be evaluated.

Provision of a smoke-free norm at work and in public places

Women need to be supported in their efforts to give up smoking by the provision of smoke-free environments in workplaces and in public places. The majority of women smokers want to give up smoking, and no-smoking policies would provide a welcome climate for cessation.

Research

It is often very difficult to obtain relevant data to inform policy directed specifically at women. The differential effects of gender should automatically be included in any research on smoking. Although this would require large (costly) samples, it is very important to consider gender differences in all research, and particularly in research on smoking cessation.

Much research has been carried out in specific groups, such as older men, without any comparisons with women. It is important to know more about the populations who are most affected: namely teenage girls and women.

A wide range of potential research could be carried out, but the following topics should be prioritised:

1   Research on the uptake of smoking, its maintenance, and prevention, in relation to girls' and women's perceptions about weight and weight control
2   More appropriate national survey data, for classifying smoking status by women's work, economic status, and ethnic group
3   Research to examine the factors underlying women's choices between cigarettes, other drugs and eating: for example, whether they use cigarettes to stop eating, whether they eat to stop smoking, and whether they drink to stop smoking and to stop eating
4   In-depth study of the socioeconomic and domestic factors affecting smoking uptake, maintenance and cessation
5   Research on the effectiveness of female-led interventions on education and cessation aimed at individuals and groups of girls and women. This would usefully inform local resource allocation.

Conclusion

In policy terms, it is important to look at the woman behind the smoker, because the 'woman smoker' does not adequately describe what is needed in terms of a policy response.

The already large policy and research agenda would benefit particularly from a more local emphasis. The National Health Service, and especially public health, now has to draw up contracts for health and health care for the local population. Directors of public health need to include smoking prevention in the local contracting system, and would benefit from a model contract for smoking policies, provisions, and intervention measures. Government support for this is needed.

This section is based on a paper prepared for the National Forum for Coronary Heart Disease Prevention by Dr Bobbie Jacobson, Director of Public Health, East London and The City Health Authority.

References

1   Graham H. 1987. Women's smoking and family health. *Social Science and Medicine*; 25: 47-56.
2   Amos A, Jacobson B, White P. 1991. Cigarette advertising policy and coverage of smoking and health in British women's magazines. *Lancet*; 337: 93-96.
3   Townsend J. 1993. Policies to halve smoking deaths. *Addiction*; 88: 43-52.
4   Townsend J. 1987. Economic and health consequences of reduced smoking. In: Williams A (ed). *Health and economics*. London: Macmillan.
5   Jacobson B. 1988. *Beating the ladykillers: women and smoking*. London: Gollancz.

CHAPTER 7

Cholesterol

Lipid levels and CHD risk in women

DAVID WOOD

SUMMARY

Women have lower total cholesterol levels than men until about age 50, after which women's levels are higher than men's. Levels of HDL cholesterol – the 'protective' cholesterol fraction – are consistently higher in women than men, although the sex difference reduces after middle age. HDL cholesterol may therefore partly explain sex differences in CHD risk. Women's triglyceride levels are lower than men's at all ages. Dietary fat (particularly saturated fat) is an important determinant of cholesterol levels. Menopause seems to cause an increase in total and LDL cholesterol, a small rise in triglycerides, and a fall in HDL cholesterol.

In women and men the risk of CHD rises as the level of cholesterol rises, but for any given cholesterol level women have a lower risk of CHD than men. The ratio of total cholesterol to HDL cholesterol may be more predictive: as the ratio increases, the CHD risk increases. It is unclear whether there is a sex difference in the relationship between triglycerides and CHD risk.

Among men, lowering blood cholesterol levels leads to a decrease in CHD incidence. However, women have not been included in any primary prevention trials. Thus, for healthy women there is no evidence to inform decisions on when and how to intervene to reduce cholesterol in an individual clinical situation, except for those with familial hyperlipidaemia. For women with CHD, there is some evidence that reducing cholesterol levels will reduce risk.

Blood lipids in women are, as for men, major determinants of coronary heart disease (CHD) risk, although the relationships are not identical.

Despite its public perception as a 'bad fat', cholesterol is essential for the structure of cell membranes and is the precursor for all steroid hormones. Most cholesterol is synthesised within the body.

A blood cholesterol measurement assesses the summation of several different fractions of cholesterol. In clinical practice and public health policy, the two lipids of major concern are cholesterol and triglyceride.

The lipoproteins come in many different forms, and have different densities, different physico-chemical properties and different functions within the body. The major lipoproteins in relation to CHD are low density lipoprotein (LDL) and high density lipoprotein (HDL). Each of these carrier lipoproteins, which comprise both fats and proteins, contains different amounts of cholesterol and triglyceride.

Distribution of lipid levels

There are now very good data on the distribution of lipids and the lipoprotein fractions in the population as a whole, which show that average lipid levels are different in different sections of the population (see Figure 1).

FIGURE 1: Blood lipid concentrations in Britain, by age and sex

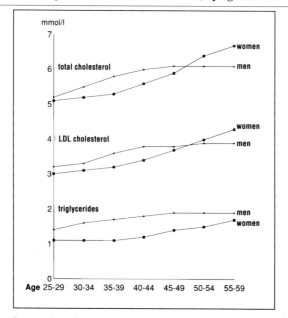

Source: See reference 1.

Total cholesterol

Figure 1 shows data for adults in the UK, and Figure 2 shows data across the lifecourse from the Lipid Research Clinic's Prevalence Study, of children and adults in the United States, from birth to over 80 years.[1, 2, 3, 4]

FIGURE 2: Distribution of plasma cholesterol in the United States, by age

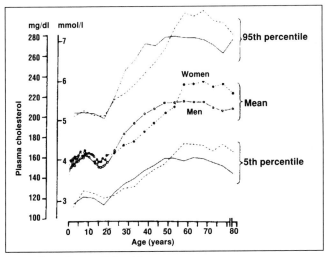

Source: See references 2,3 and 4.

Early in life, total cholesterol rises quite rapidly, and then falls during puberty. Throughout adulthood, total cholesterol level rises with age in both women and men, and only starts to fall again when people are in their 60s.

Average levels for girls and boys are similar. In early adulthood, however, a sex difference appears, and women have lower average total cholesterol levels than men until the age of about 50. At this time, women's average total cholesterol level rises quite substantially and remains greater than that of men for the rest of life.

LDL cholesterol

Low density lipoprotein (LDL) is the principal cholesterol-carrying lipoprotein. Levels of LDL cholesterol follow a similar pattern to that of total cholesterol, rising with age in both sexes during adult life, until people are in their 60s. LDL cholesterol levels are consistently lower (and better) in women than in men until about the age of 50, when a crossover occurs. (See Figure 1).

HDL cholesterol

High density lipoprotein (HDL) cholesterol is the protective cholesterol fraction. Figure 3 shows levels of plasma HDL cholesterol over the lifecourse, for both women and men. Average levels of HDL cholesterol are consistently higher in women than in men, throughout adult life, although this sex difference is reduced after middle age. HDL cholesterol may therefore partly explain the sex differences in CHD risk.

FIGURE 3: Distribution of plasma HDL cholesterol in the United States, by age

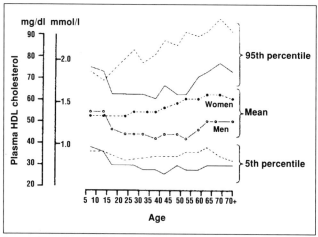

Source: See references 2,3 and 4.

Ratio of total cholesterol to HDL cholesterol

In both sexes, the ratio of total cholesterol to HDL cholesterol rises progressively with age, but is lower at every age in women compared to men.

Triglycerides

Triglycerides show much greater variability than cholesterol, particularly if measured in non-fasting samples. Triglyceride levels rise with age in women, although women's average triglyceride levels are consistently lower than those in men at all ages. The sex difference is most marked in middle age, and disappears during the later years of life (see Figure 1).

Factors influencing lipid levels

There is considerable variation in lipid levels, influenced by a variety of factors, and it is important that this variation is taken into account.

Biological variability

If cholesterol is measured in the same individual repeatedly over several days, the results will be different, even after allowing for measurement error at the laboratory. The coefficient of biological variation is about 5%.

Seasonal variation

Cholesterol tends to rise in winter and fall in summer. This may in part reflect a change in diet, but also a change in body weight, as individuals become heavier in winter and lighter in summer.

Illness

Illness may reduce lipoproteins in the circulation. After surgery, trauma or myocardial infarction, for example, lipoprotein levels may fall by as much as 50%. Other diseases, such as hypothyroidism or renal disease, can lead to an increase in levels.

Diet

Dietary fat, and particularly saturated fat, is an important determinant of cholesterol levels. A 10% change in the proportion of energy derived from saturated fat calories leads to a change of 1 mmol/l in blood cholesterol level in the same direction.[5] The effect of polyunsaturated fats is about half that of saturated fats, in the opposite direction. Thus, an increase in the proportion of fat derived from polyunsaturated fat leads to a fall in blood cholesterol. The contribution of monounsaturated fats to lipoprotein levels is still under debate. Evidence suggests that monounsaturated fats, and in particular oleic acid, may be associated with slightly lower cholesterol levels.

Dietary cholesterol is not an important determinant of blood cholesterol. However, there is much confusion among the general public between dietary and blood cholesterol, and about the nature of a 'low cholesterol diet' – which would probably be better termed a (blood) cholesterol-lowering diet.

Alcohol consumption is also associated with an increase in HDL cholesterol. The effect of coffee, particularly boiled coffee, on cholesterol, is debatable.

Hormones and the effect of the menopause

In women, cholesterol levels are also affected by hormones. Within the menstrual cycle, cholesterol level reaches a peak at ovulation, and falls at the time of menstruation. Profound rises in lipoproteins, particularly cholesterol and triglycerides, also occur during pregnancy, reaching a peak just before birth. Both the oral contraceptive pill and hormone replacement therapy (HRT) can also influence lipoprotein levels.

Menopause appears to have an unfavourable effect on lipoprotein metabolism. At menopause, levels of total cholesterol and LDL cholesterol increase, there is a smaller increase in triglyerides, and HDL cholesterol decreases. Among women receiving HRT, some of these changes may be ameliorated (see Chapter 9).

Physical activity

Physical activity seems to have little effect on total cholesterol levels, but a positive effect on HDL cholesterol. This benefit has been found both in endurance-trained women and in women who take more moderate amounts of exercise. (For further information see *How physical activity affects lipoprotein metabolism* in Chapter 10.)

Weight

Heavier women have higher levels of blood cholesterol and triglycerides, but overall there is a relatively weak correlation between body weight and total blood cholesterol level. In people with a Body Mass Index (BMI) of under 20 to about 27, the increase in blood cholesterol level is quite steep. However, in people with BMIs of 27 or above, it begins to plateau at about 6.4 mmol/l. The effect is similar in both women and men.

In the UK, even the thinnest men may have very high average blood cholesterol levels by international standards, and this is probably also true for women. Among middle-aged men in the British Regional Heart Study, those in the lowest 5% of BMI, that is the very thin men, had an average blood cholesterol level of 5.8 mmol/l.

Weight reduction, however it is achieved, will lead to a fall in cholesterol. Longitudinal data from the Framingham study has indicated that a loss of weight in individuals was associated with a decrease in blood cholesterol levels and a decrease in blood pressure much greater than would be expected from cross-sectional studies. However, the greatest fall in cholesterol is achieved through a reduction in saturated fat in the diet.

Measuring cholesterol levels

Cholesterol measurements are taken by many different methods, some of which have not been validated. The precision and accuracy of the measurement are important for informing management decisions. Cholesterol measuring methods have been developed commercially for use in the office or the out-patient clinic, or for sale in supermarkets. However, these may not have the same level of standardisation as laboratory methods: the precision and accuracy of such measurements are therefore open to question. Furthermore, although the fasting state is not important for measuring total cholesterol, it is important for triglyceride measurement.

Lipids and CHD risk

In both women and men, the risk of CHD increases as the level of total cholesterol rises, although in younger women a rise in risk is only apparent for cholesterol levels over 6.8 mmol/l. Thus, on average, the higher the cholesterol level, the higher the risk of CHD (see Table 1). However, for any given cholesterol level, women have a lower risk of CHD than men, at all ages. The relative risk is greatest for younger women and falls with increasing age.

TABLE 1: Total cholesterol and risk of CHD

	Annual incidence rate of CHD/1,000			
Total cholesterol	Women		Men	
mmol/l	**35-64**	**65-94**	**35-64**	**65-94**
<5.3	4	11	8	22
5.3-6.0	5	15	13	24
6.1-6.8	4	17	14	26
6.9-7.6	7	17	15	23
>7.6	10	21	26	38

Source: See reference 6.

The relationship between the cholesterol fractions and CHD risk is stronger, particularly for HDL cholesterol. LDL cholesterol is positively associated with the risk of CHD: the higher the LDL cholesterol level, the higher the risk of CHD. HDL cholesterol is inversely and independently associated with CHD risk: the higher the HDL cholesterol level, the lower the CHD risk. However, the association of HDL cholesterol with CHD risk is twice as strong in women aged over 50 years. The relationship between triglyceride and CHD risk is less clear, and it remains uncertain whether there is a sex difference in this relationship.

The predictive power of the lipoprotein fractions for CHD risk is strengthened when they are assessed together. In particular, the ratio of total cholesterol to HDL cholesterol has a stronger predictive power for CHD incidence than total cholesterol alone. The risk of CHD increases as this ratio increases, in both women and men[7] (see Table 2). As the ratio of total cholesterol:HDL cholesterol rises in women, so the risk of CHD approaches that of men. There is no difference in risk between the sexes in those with the highest ratio.

TABLE 2: Total:HDL cholesterol ratio and risk of CHD

Age adjusted incidence of CHD/1,000

Total:HDL cholesterol ratio	Women	Men
<3.5	34	70
3.5-5.4	56	95
5.5-7.4	78	152
7.5-9.4	171	176
≥9.5	281	275

Source: See reference 7.

Lowering cholesterol levels

Evidence from clinical trials involving men clearly shows that lowering blood cholesterol levels leads to a reduction in the incidence of CHD.[8] For a 10% reduction in cholesterol, there is an average 18% reduction in CHD risk, and this relationship holds true for primary and secondary prevention trials, and trials using either diet or drugs. Women have not been included in any primary prevention trials and thus there is no evidence on the effects of cholesterol reduction among healthy women. However, the three secondary prevention trials with separate data on women indicate that cholesterol reduction is associated with a significant reduction in CHD risk, similar in size to that found among men in the same studies. As yet there is no evidence for either women or men that lowering cholesterol reduces total all-cause mortality.

The comparative lack of scientific data for women has important implications for advice on the management of cholesterol and its subfractions, and other CHD risk factors in women. In order to justify diagnostic tests in health care, clear management policies are needed on how the results will be used. For healthy women, there is currently no evidence to inform decisions about when and how to intervene to reduce cholesterol in an individual clinical situation, except for those with familial hyperlipidaemia. However, the evidence from the few trials which included women suggests that, when a woman has developed CHD, cholesterol lowering is associated with a similar reduction in the risk of CHD to that seen in men.

This section is based on a paper prepared for the National Forum for Coronary Heart Disease Prevention by Professor David Wood, Honorary Consultant Cardiologist at the National Heart and Lung Institute. Professor Wood represents the British Cardiac Society on the Forum.

References

1   Mann JI, Lewis B, Shepherd J, Winder AF, Fenster S, Rose L, Morgan B. 1988. Blood lipid concentrations and other cardiovascular risk factors: distribution, prevalence and detection in Britain. *British Medical Journal*; 296: 1702-1706.

2   Lipid Research Clinics Program Epidemiology Committee. 1979. Plasma lipid distributions in selected North American populations: The Lipid Research Clinics Program Prevalence Study. *Circulation*; 60: 427-439.

3   Heiss G, Tamir I, Davis CE, Tyroler HA, Rifkind BM, Schonfeld G, Jacobs D, Frantz ID. 1988. Lipoprotein cholesterol distributions in selected North American populations: The Lipid Research Clinics Program Prevalence Study. *Circulation*; 61: 302-315.

4   Heiss G, Johnson NJ, Reiland S, Davis CE, Tyroler JA. 1980. The epidemiology of plasma high-density lipoprotein cholesterol levels. The Lipid Research Clinics Program Prevalence Study Summary. *Circulation*; 62 (Suppl. IV): 116-136.

5   Hegsted DM, McGundy RB, Myers ML, Stare FJ. 1965. Quantitative effects of dietary fat on serum cholesterol in man. *American Journal of Clinical Nutrition*; 17: 281-295.

6   Cupples LA, D'Agostino RB, Kiely T. 1987. Some risk factors related to the annual incidence of cardiovascular disease and death. Framingham Study. 30-year follow-up. *National Institute of Health Publication; 87-2703.* US Department of Commerce, National Technical Information Service, Washington, DC.

7   Kannel WB. 1983. High density lipoproteins: epidemiologic profile and risks of coronary artery disease. *American Journal of Cardiology*; 51: 93-123.

8   Law MR, Wald NJ, Thompson SG. 1994. By how much and how quickly does reduction in serum cholesterol concentration lower risk of ischaemic heart disease? *British Medical Journal*; 308: 367-372.

Cholesterol levels in women: what are the policy implications?

HUGH TUNSTALL-PEDOE

SUMMARY

The majority of people aged over 40 with high cholesterol levels in the UK are women. In younger age groups cholesterol levels are lower in women than men but, by the age of 55, the majority of women in the UK have levels over 6.5 mmol/l and about one-third have levels over 7.8 mmol/l. Much of the high total cholesterol levels in older women is accounted for by higher HDL cholesterol levels.

The differences between women and men in lipid levels and CHD risk have no special implications for a population approach: strategies to promote a healthy diet and physical activity, and to reduce smoking and obesity, are important for all. However, the differences in cholesterol levels have considerable implications for a high risk approach linked to individual risk factor assessment. Guidelines incorporating fixed cut-points for total cholesterol and which take no account of age and sex are inappropriate and impractical, and would result in referral of huge numbers of women to lipid clinics.* They may also result in women inappropriately being given lipid-lowering drugs, the advantages and safety of which have not been demonstrated in large-scale trials among women.

Management of individual risk should be based on an integrated approach to risk factor assessment. Cholesterol measurements should not be made or interpreted without taking account of age and sex and integrating them with other risk factors, such as smoking and blood pressure, into an overall score.

An effective national nutrition policy is needed to address the high cholesterol levels in the UK: without it, individual cholesterol measurements will not secure change.

* See footnote on page 102.

The risk of coronary heart disease (CHD) is considerably lower in women than in men, at all ages, and, although rates among women are nearer to those in men in old age, they never catch up. Conventional wisdom holds that rates in women accelerate after the menopause, as a protective effect is removed. However, among both women and men, the rate of rise in CHD mortality decelerates with increasing age, and this deceleration is more marked in men (see Figure 1 on page 58). If a protective effect *is* removed in women and there are risk factors which increase at the time of menopause, they do not appear to have any effect. Perhaps there are others which change in the opposite direction.

Coronary heart disease trends among women and men in the same countries show a strong correlation, suggesting that similar causes are operating in both sexes (see *International differences* in Chapter 5). Many studies suggest that the relative risk and the weighting of CHD risk factors in women are likely to be the same as those in men.[1] However, women have been comparatively neglected in research studies on CHD, and many studies have not included women. Among men, the definitive study of smoking, blood pressure and cholesterol was the Multiple Risk Factor Intervention Trial,[2] which involved 325,000 men. To produce similar results among women would need a study involving 1-2 million women.

The sex difference in CHD incidence has implications for prevention strategies directed at women and men, including interventions aimed at lowering cholesterol levels. Although the relative risk of CHD associated with total cholesterol may be similar in both sexes, the absolute risk of CHD in women is lower than in men. This means that cost-benefit, and risk-benefit, calculations for women and men will produce different answers.

Cholesterol levels among women and men

The majority of people over age 40 with high cholesterol levels in the UK are women. The effect of age on levels in women is dramatic. At younger ages, blood cholesterol levels are lower in women than in men. However, average cholesterol levels increase throughout adult life and, after age 50, become increasingly higher in women than in men. At age 25, a small minority of women have high cholesterol levels. By age 55, however, the majority of women in the UK have levels above 6.5 mmol/l and about a third have levels over 7.8 mmol/l. This is illustrated by data on serum cholesterol from the Scottish Heart Health and Scottish MONICA studies.[3] These show that, among men, cholesterol levels are relatively stable from age 35 to 65, and among women, they rise steeply (see Figures 1 and 2).

Such changes over the lifespan are not specific to the UK, to overweight populations, or to countries with high cholesterol levels, but occur in all populations studied in the WHO MONICA population surveys, including countries with low cholesterol levels such as China.[4]

Blood cholesterol levels in women are not only *quantitatively* different at each age from those in men, but are also *qualitatively* different. Average levels of the protective high density lipoprotein (HDL) cholesterol are higher in women, and increase with age, and much of the high average total cholesterol level in older women is accounted for by their higher HDL cholesterol levels. The proportion of total cholesterol from non-HDL cholesterol is therefore lower in women than in men.[5,6] The implication of the higher HDL cholesterol levels among women are: either that a total cholesterol reading has to be interpreted in the context of age and sex; or (a more expensive option) that HDL cholesterol should also be measured in women when total cholesterol is measured, as recommended in some guidelines.[7]

Policy implications

The differences between women and men in absolute levels of coronary risk, and in their blood cholesterol levels and fractions, have no special implications for the population approach to coronary prevention. A healthy diet is not only potentially beneficial in reducing coronary risk, but may also benefit other common causes of morbidity and mortality. There is no reason why a diet with less saturated fat and more complex carbohydrates, micronutrients and fibre, should be anything other than beneficial for both sexes.

However, the implications of the sex differences for the high risk approach, linked to individual risk factor assessment, are considerable. The most widely recommended guidelines for cholesterol management in the UK for many years were those published in 1987 by the European Atherosclerosis Society (EAS)[8] which were based on research among men and made no distinction between the sexes.* These guidelines advocated that individuals with a cholesterol level above 6.5 mmol/l should be under clinical care, and those over 7.8 mmol/l should be referred to a lipid clinic.

Such 'guidelines' would result in 40% of 35-64 year old men in the UK being under clinical care and about 9% being referred to a lipid clinic. There is little variation in cholesterol levels between these ages, so the percentages remain similar throughout this age group.

For women, however, the situation is rather different. Over 75% of women aged 55-64 would be under clinical care (having a total cholesterol level above 6.5 mmol/l) and 31% would be referred to a lipid clinic (with levels over 7.8

See footnote on next page.

mmol/l).

Although the risk of CHD is much lower among women than among men of the same age, the original EAS guidelines implied that more than three times as many women aged 55-64 should be referred to lipid clinics than men.

One of the requirements for a screening programme is a clear idea of what action will be taken on the basis of the results. For women, high blood cholesterol is associated with a lower risk of CHD than in men, and the advantages and safety of lipid-lowering drugs have not been demonstrated in large scale trials among women. Furthermore, lipid levels may be modified by menopausal status or hormone replacement therapy, opening up a different dimension of management. These problems have now been acknowledged in the guidelines of the British Hyperlipidaemia Association,[7,9] who advise caution in extending lipid lowering treatment to women.

This illustrates the problem of extrapolating a set of guidelines from studies carried out in men, across to women, without adequate justification. The use of fixed cut-points is a doubtful practice at any age. The chosen cut-points resulted in the stigmatisation of huge numbers of middle-aged women for clinical care, or specialist referral. Furthermore, the increase in total cholesterol with age in women produces bizarre results, which were not addressed in the guidelines.

The original EAS guidelines for cholesterol management were neither rational nor feasible and, although they have been widely publicised to GPs, there can have been few GPs who accepted them, and few lipid clinics able to cope with referral of nearly 10% of their local middle-aged population. The guidelines have been amended twice[10,11] but, despite more discussion of the multifactorial nature of CHD risk and the sex differences, and acknowledgement that women's lower incidence of CHD at younger ages should be taken into account in therapy, the fundamental cut-points for intervention have *not* been changed. Furthermore, the guidelines do not take into account the steep rise and higher cholesterol levels among post-menopausal women.* There is, however, greater interest in measuring HDL cholesterol among women, although an alternative would be to measure lipids *only* if there were strong specific indications.

---

*   *Since this critique of the cut-point approach to total cholesterol was first mounted in 1989 (see reference 3), the bodies responsible for issuing the original guidelines have progressively taken into account the criticisms. A new set of guidelines, which acknowledge the sex and age differences in cholesterol, blood pressure and CHD risk, were published by the European Society of Cardiology, the European Atherosclerosis Society and the European Society of Hypertension as this report went to press (see reference 18). The critique outlined in this chapter remains important in emphasising that an approach which takes cholesterol readings out of context and which ignores the differences between women and men is not acceptable.*

The charts in Figures 1 and 2 aid interpretation of serum cholesterol readings in Britain. To use them, read up vertically from the patient's cholesterol until you reach the curve for that age and then read the percentage from the vertical scale. The 50% line is the average.

FIGURE 1: How-often-that-high: cholesterol levels among Scottish women

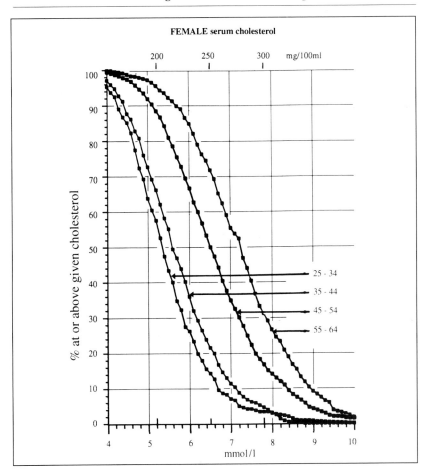

Source: See reference 3.

FIGURE 2 : How-often-that-high: cholesterol levels among Scottish men

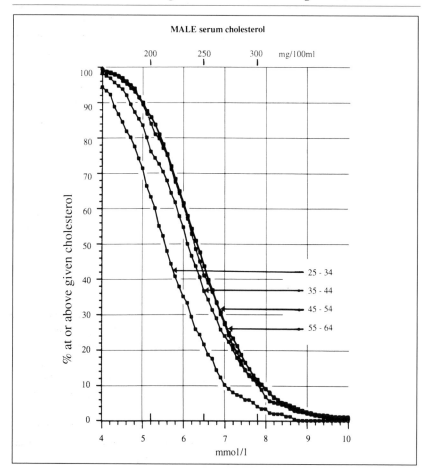

Source: See reference 3.

An integrated approach to risk factor assessment

An integrated approach to risk factor management is more appropriate than using single factor guidelines. A combined risk factor score could, at its simplest, include smoking, blood pressure and blood cholesterol.[12, 13] In the Scottish population, where cigarette smoking levels among the two sexes are almost equal, the distribution of such a combined risk factor score is almost identical among women and men aged 40-59. Without compensation for sex differences in risk factor levels however, the score in women increases with age, whereas that for men is more stable between these ages.

The Dundee Coronary Risk-Disk is a circular slide-rule which provides a rapid assessment of the score, and gives a ranking from 1 (most risk) to 100 (least risk) based on equal hundredths of the population. The rise in cholesterol and blood pressure with increasing age in women is compensated by a staggered start, so that the ranking takes age and sex into account. The ranking gives the individual a sense of their coronary risk in relation to the rest of the population: it tells them whether their modifiable risk factors place them below or above average risk. It may motivate change, and offers a means of monitoring progress. It therefore provides a basis for a high-risk approach to coronary prevention applicable to both sexes.[14]

The Risk-Disk can be used with or without cholesterol measurement. The provisional ranking, made without cholesterol measurement, can be used to decide whether a cholesterol test is justified. However, the relative ranking in relation to age and sex is not an absolute indication of risk. A 60 year old man is at greater risk than a 40 year old woman with the same smoking, blood pressure and cholesterol levels.

Cholesterol testing

Two prevalent misconceptions about blood cholesterol results are even more inappropriate to women than men. One is that high blood cholesterol inevitably means high coronary risk (before integrating the result with other risk factors). The second is that a blood cholesterol level above 7.8 mmol/l denotes a genetic abnormality. Among 55-64 year old women the prevalence of such levels is 31%: 150 times greater than the presumed gene frequency for familial hypercholesterolaemia.

Cholesterol measurements should not therefore be made or interpreted by those who are unaware of the distribution of cholesterol by age and sex (see Figures 1 and 2). If measured at all, they need to be integrated into a score of modifiable coronary risk.

The justifications for cholesterol testing are to identify those who may need drug treatment, to aid overall risk assessment, and to motivate dietary change. Decisions on drug treatment are usually based on the presence of other factors and these have led to a standard list of unifactorial indications for cholesterol measurement[14] such as: a family history of CHD; skin and eye manifestations of raised cholesterol; having manifestations of cardiovascular disease or diabetes; or being already under care for or having had surgery for these diseases. Overall assessment implies evaluation of other factors and these can be done first, leaving a decision on cholesterol to depend again on the importance of other factors. These are arguments for selective testing.[15, 16]

Evidence that cholesterol test results motivate dietary change is – despite all the enthusiasm – largely anecdotal and based on clinical impression. At least one study suggests that the motivation in those identified as having above average cholesterol may be counter-balanced by inertia in those who are identified as average, when what is needed is change at almost all levels.[17] Blood cholesterol is a risk factor specific for CHD. As the risk of CHD is lower in women, any cost-benefit arguments for cholesterol testing are correspondingly diluted.

However, whether selective or mass cholesterol testing is undertaken in individuals, there is a need for good population data on levels and trends of coronary risk factors, including blood cholesterol, measured in a standardised manner. These need to be collected regularly at national and regional levels and on a sufficient scale to monitor what is happening to the increasingly heterogeneous components of the population.

The need for a national nutrition policy

A national nutrition policy is needed to address the population's high blood cholesterol levels. Without an effective national nutrition policy, and a corresponding change in diet, individual cholesterol measurements will not secure change. A national nutrition policy can reinforce the high risk strategy, and vice versa. However, a high risk strategy in the absence of a national nutrition policy means that the primary care team will be extremely disappointed with the results of their counselling.

The UK has a food policy but not a nutrition policy. In Europe, the Common Agricultural Policy governs price and availability of food but is designed more for the interests of the producers than for the health of the consumers. It would be difficult to secure a national nutrition policy without also securing a change of heart in the European Union. The Health of the Nation Nutrition Task Force in England, and any Scottish equivalent, need to address this issue.

Conclusion

The differences in lipid levels and of coronary risk between women and men have no major implications for a population strategy for CHD prevention. Advice given to the population about a healthy diet, overweight, physical activity and smoking applies equally to both sexes. Such lifestyle changes are unlikely to have any negative impact on other major women-specific diseases such as breast cancer.

There is a need for a national nutrition policy which can be applied to the whole adult population regardless of age and sex, to counter – among other things – the high lipid levels in the population.

However, the differences in cholesterol patterns between the sexes do have implications for the high risk strategy and intervention on the individual level. Allowances must be made both for the lower absolute level of risk, and for cholesterol changes with age in women.

The majority of individuals over 40 with high cholesterol levels in the UK are women. The effect of age on cholesterol levels in women is dramatic. Cholesterol levels should not be measured unless they can be interpreted, using for example, the *How-often-that-high graphs* (see Figures 1 and 2). Male cut-points are inappropriate for women, and their use is likely to cause much anxiety to older women. Lipids should be assessed in relation to age and sex, as well as the presence or absence of other risk factors, and a composite score, which corrects for age and sex differences, should be used in assessing the CHD risk in women.

If CHD risk factor screening is to be carried out in women, health professionals will need to be educated on the problem of interpreting women's cholesterol levels. Naive guidelines, based on fixed cut-points, which take no account of differing levels of cholesterol and of risk in women, are inappropriate.

This section is based on a paper prepared for the National Forum for Coronary Heart Disease Prevention by Professor Hugh Tunstall-Pedoe, Director of the Cardiovascular Epidemiology Unit, University of Dundee. Professor Tunstall-Pedoe is an individual member of the Forum.

References

1   Isles CG, Hole DJ, Hawthorne VM, Lever AF. 1992. Relation between coronary risk and coronary mortality in women of the Renfrew and Paisley survey: comparison with men. *Lancet*; 339: 702-706.

2   Kannel WB, Neaton JD, Wentworth D et al. 1986. Overall and coronary heart disease mortality rates in relation to major risk factors in 325,348 men screened for MRFIT. *American Heart Journal*; 112: 825-836.

3   Tunstall-Pedoe H, Smith WCS, Tavendale R. 1989. How-often-that-high graphs of serum cholesterol. Findings from the Scottish Heart Health and Scottish MONICA studies. *Lancet*; i: 540-542.

4   World Health Organization. 1989. *The WHO MONICA Project: a worldwide monitoring system for cardiovascular diseases.* World Health Statistics Annual 1989.

5   Smith WCS, Tunstall-Pedoe H, Crombie IK, Tavendale R. 1989. Concomitants of excess coronary deaths – major risk factor and lifestyle findings from 10,359 men and women in the Scottish Heart Health Study. *Scottish Medical Journal*; 34: 550-555.

6   The Lipid Research Clinics Program Epidemiology Committee. 1979. Plasma lipid distributions in selected North American populations: The Lipid Research Clinics Program Prevalence Study. *Circulation*; 60: 427-439.

7   Durrington P. 1993. Summary and British Hyperlipidaemia Association guidelines. In:

Laker MF, Neil A, Wood C (eds). *Cholesterol lowering trials: advice for the British physician*. London: Royal College of Physicians of London.

8   European Atherosclerosis Society Study Group. 1987. Strategies for the prevention of coronary heart disease: a policy statement of the European Atherosclerosis Society. *European Heart Journal*; 9: 77-88.

9   Betteridge DJ, Dodson PM, Durrington PN, Hughes EA, Laker MF et al. 1993. Management of hyperlipidaemia: guidelines of the British Hyperlipidaemia Association. *Postgraduate Medical Journal*; 69: 359-369.

10   European Atherosclerosis Society Study Group. 1988. The recognition and management of hyperlipidaemia in adults: a policy statement of the European Atherosclerosis Society. *European Heart Journal*; 9: 571-600.

11   European Atherosclerosis Society International Task Force for Prevention of Coronary Heart Disease. 1992. Prevention of coronary heart disease: scientific background and new clinical guidelines. *Nutrition, Metabolism and Cardiovascular Diseases*; 2: 113-156.

12   Tunstall-Pedoe H. 1991. The Dundee coronary risk-disk for management of change in risk factors. *British Medical Journal*; 303: 744-747.

13   Tunstall-Pedoe H. 1992. Value of the Dundee coronary risk-disk: a defence. *British Medical Journal*; 305: 231-232.

14   Working Group of the Coronary Prevention Group and the British Heart Foundation. 1991. An action plan for preventing coronary heart disease in primary care. *British Medical Journal*; 303: 748-750.

15   Tunstall-Pedoe H. 1989. Who is for cholesterol testing? *British Medical Journal*; 298: 1593-1594.

16   Consensus statement. 1989. *Blood cholesterol measurement in the prevention of coronary heart disease*. Sixth King's Fund Forum: King Edward's Hospital Fund for London. London: King's Fund.

17   Kinlay S, Heller RF. 1990. Effectiveness and hazards of case finding for high cholesterol concentration. *British Medical Journal*; 300: 1545-1547.

18   Pyorala K, De Backer G, Graham I, Poole-Wilson P, Wood D, on behalf of the Task Force. 1994. Prevention of coronary heart disease in clinical practice: Recommendations of the Task Force of the European Society of Cardiology, European Atherosclerosis Society and European Society of Hypertension. *European Heart Journal*; 15: 1300-1331.

CHAPTER 8

Diet

Diet and CHD:
are there special issues for women?

PHILIP JAMES

SUMMARY

Women in the UK, like men, eat a very high fat diet. They have a higher intake of saturated fat as a percentage of energy than men, and a lower average P:S ratio. There is a causal relationship between saturated fatty acids and cholesterol levels. The effects of individual fatty acids are being re-examined, which has implications for recommendations on diet. Women's fibre intake is lower than men's and the cholesterol-lowering effect of fibre may be less marked in women.

There is growing evidence that increased levels of antioxidants such as vitamins C and E, and beta-carotene, found primarily in fruit and vegetables, may protect against CHD. However, fruit and vegetable consumption is very low among UK women, as among men. Iron stores may promote atherosclerosis: if so, pre-menopausal women may be protected by their lower iron status.

Obesity is an important determinant of CHD risk in women, and there has been a large increase in obesity in women in the UK. Waist:hip ratio may be a better predictor of CHD risk: women tend to have lower ratios than men. There is a synergistic effect between obesity and other CHD risk factors, particularly smoking and diabetes. Prevention of obesity, and of CHD, should begin in childhood.

International comparisons show that women have different rates of coronary heart disease (CHD) in different countries, strongly implying substantial environmental factors. There is a strong synergistic effect between the different risk factors for CHD, such as raised blood cholesterol, raised blood pressure and cigarette smoking.[1]

Many of the issues concerning diet and CHD affect both women and men, and a nutrition strategy aimed at the whole population is likely to be effective for both sexes. However, there are also some special issues for women.

The impact of different fatty acids on CHD

Average cholesterol levels are very high among British women. Data from The Dietary and Nutritional Survey of British Adults[2] show that, in the UK, about 90% of women in their 50s have cholesterol levels above the European Atherosclerosis Society cut-off point of 5.2 mmol/l (see Chapter 7).

Until recently, British women had a diet that was higher in fat than that of men. Their intake of saturated fatty acids, as a percentage of food energy, is still higher, their intake of polyunsaturated fatty acids is slightly lower, and women have a lower average P:S ratio (ratio of polyunsaturates to saturates) than men.[2]

The Seven Countries study[3] showed the direct relationship between saturated fatty acids in the diet and serum cholesterol, among men. Unfortunately, there are no comparable data for women. However, many studies in both women and men, including physiological studies, show very clearly that there is a causal link between saturated fatty acids in the diet and blood cholesterol levels.

For 40 years, the focus has been on saturated fatty acids, and nutritional guidance has recommended a reduction in saturates. In the attempt to portray a simple message, total saturated and total polyunsaturated fats have been commonly considered when trying to delineate the principal factors which link to an increase in cholesterol. The Keys formula[4] shows that a change in saturated fatty acid has roughly twice the impact of the change in polyunsaturated fatty acid on total serum cholesterol, but in the reverse direction. An increase in saturated fat intake increases blood cholesterol, and an increase in polyunsaturates decreases blood cholesterol.

Some of the complexity of diet in the aetiology of CHD has been summarised by Ulbricht and Southgate,[5] who point out that CHD involves two pathological effects – atheroma and thrombogenesis – and that dietary factors are implicated in different ways. They argue that the saturated and polyunsaturated fat message, and in particular the P:S ratio, are too simplistic, and emphasise the need to consider the different promotional or protective properties of the individual fatty acids in relation to the two principal contributors to the obstruction of coronary vessels – atherosclerosis and thrombosis (blood clotting). They have examined the impact of the different fatty acids on blood cholesterol[5] and have compiled an 'index of atherogenicity' and an 'index of thrombogenicity' based on the different impact of the individual saturated, polyunsaturated and monounsaturated fatty acids on blood cholesterol.

It is clear from earlier data that the individual fatty acids each have a different impact on blood cholesterol. Keys[4] had originally suggested that the saturated fatty acids, lauric acid (C12), myristic acid (C14) and palmitic acid (C16), effectively had the same impact on increasing cholesterol, and that polyunsaturated fatty acids (PUFAs) such as linoleic acid (C18:2) decreased cholesterol. Hegsted,[6] however, suggested that myristic acid (C14) had the most important impact on blood cholesterol and was therefore most atherogenic.

Atherogenesis

The 'index of atherogenicity' developed by Ulbricht and Southgate is based on the dietary intake of lauric acid, myristic acid, palmitic acid, polyunsaturated fatty acids, oleic acid and other monounsaturates. It seems that myristic acid is the main fatty acid responsible for raising LDL cholesterol levels – important in atheroma. It also seems clear now that myristic and lauric acid also suppress the clearing mechanisms which remove LDL cholesterol from circulation, and in that way also have a direct impact in raising LDL cholesterol levels.

There is some controversy about the effect of the saturated palmitic acid: however, palm oil seems to raise cholesterol levels less than the usual mix of fats consumed in the western diet.

Thus myristic acid and lauric acid seem to be the two most atherogenic saturated fatty acids. The net effect is that particular fats such as coconut oil, milk, butter and cheese, which tend to contain a lot of lauric and myristic acid, make the diet more atherogenic by increasing LDL cholesterol levels.

Thrombogenesis

Ulbricht and Southgate[5] have also emphasised that the different fatty acids seem to have different impacts on thrombogenesis, and the 'index of thrombogenicity' reflects this. Thus stearic acid seems to promote thrombosis but not atherogenesis. Myristic acid also contributes to the development of thrombosis. Dairy products seem to be the most thrombogenic component of the British diet, followed by palm oil and most meats. Monounsaturated fatty acids, seed oils and fish oils may protect against thrombosis.

Research also suggests that trans-fatty acids, produced during the hydrogenation of oils, may be important in increasing thrombogenesis as well as increasing LDL cholesterol and reducing HDL cholesterol levels in the blood.[7] If true, this would have enormous implications for the food industry, which uses processes that produce trans-fatty acids.

The total amount of fat in the diet may also be important in thrombogenesis.

Miller,[8] for example, found that the total amount of fat in the diet increases Factor VII, one of the factors involved in blood clotting.

Polyunsaturated and monounsaturated fatty acids
Understanding of the effect of the different unsaturated fatty acids – polyunsaturated and monounsaturated fatty acids – on CHD risk has been confused by the different effects of polyunsaturated and monounsaturated fatty acid intakes when studied on liquid formula diets as distinct from normal diets.

In individuals on normal diets, polyunsaturated fatty acids have a greater impact on lowering LDL cholesterol than monounsaturated fatty acids do. This is probably because they increase the removal of LDL cholesterol from the circulation, while monounsaturates do not. It is possible that the liquid formula diet has exaggerated the positive 'value' of monounsaturated fatty acids. Since almost all the studies have been conducted on liquid formula diets, some of the supposed benefits of monounsaturated fatty acids need to be re-evaluated.[9]

There is therefore conflicting evidence on the role of monounsaturated fatty acids. Khosla and Hayes[10,11] have re-evaluated the effects of individual fatty acids experimentally, and shown that oleic acid increases the production of VLDL cholesterol, but does not lead to increases in LDL cholesterol because it also induces an increase in the clearance rate of LDL cholesterol.

Furthermore, cross-cultural studies on CHD in relation to monounsaturates in olive oil are complicated by the additional components in olive oil, such as antioxidants, and by other associated dietary features, such as vegetable consumption.

Fibre

A fall in serum cholesterol can usually be produced by increasing vegetable and fruit intake. The fibre intake in a normal diet promotes cholesterol removal from the body. Dietary fibre may also promote the cholesterol-lowering effects of polyunsaturated fatty acids. However, the total non-starch polysaccharide (NSP) or fibre intake of women is lower than men and at equivalent intakes women have a smaller faecal output. Thus women may be particularly vulnerable to the effects of low fibre intake, and the cholesterol-lowering effect of fibre may be less marked in women.

Although cereal fibre does not usually have a metabolic effect in reducing blood cholesterol levels, the consumption of cereal fibre may also protect individuals against CHD for reasons that are unclear. Part of the effect of a high fibre diet, rich in cereals and vegetables, in preventing CHD, may also relate to its other effects, such as the lowering of blood pressure seen in people on a vegetarian diet.[12]

A high fibre diet also results in higher oestrogen levels in the faeces, and leads to a reduction in circulating oestrogen levels, but the full effect of fibre sources on the sex hormone metabolism of women has not been evaluated.

A high vegetable, cereal and fruit intake may thus have a multiplicity of metabolic effects: it does not operate through a single selective process.

Antioxidants

There is growing evidence that increased levels of antioxidants such as vitamins C and E, and beta-carotene, found primarily in fresh fruit and vegetables, may protect against CHD.

The classic indices of risk in relation to diet are currently being modified. There is now a recognition that free radical reactions, which cause cellular damage, are very important in the development of atheroma. Furthermore, free iron is recognised to promote the generation of free radicals, so interest has also centred on whether an individual's iron status might affect the development of CHD. Thus it is possible that iron stores in the body may promote the oxidation of lipoproteins – mediated by free radicals – and thereby atherosclerosis. If so, pre-menopausal women may be protected in part from CHD by their poor iron status. Free radical reactions are inhibited by antioxidant nutrients such as vitamin C and vitamin E, and therefore these vitamins may well prove to be protective.

If antioxidants are powerful protectors against CHD, then the sex differences in the trends of CHD since the 1950s, with women's rates falling while men's rates rose, may reflect the widespread emphasis on slimming diets among women. These diets promoted the consumption of fruit and salads, and therefore antioxidant nutrients.

The World Health Organization recommends that all adults should eat at least five portions of fruit and vegetables a day.[13] Fruit and vegetable consumption among both women and men in the UK is very low, and in some groups less than half of that recommended.

Women are increasing their fruit consumption, but their vegetable consumption is still very low. British women are more likely than men to eat fruit and, in Scotland, women are more likely than men to eat green vegetables. The estimated vitamin C intake of women is as great as that of men, despite their lower overall food intake. Male smokers also consume less vitamin C than non-smokers. It is likely that the same is true for women.[14] This is particularly important, as heavy smoking may double or treble the normal vitamin C requirements, reflecting the marked impact of free radicals in cigarette smoke.

This difference in vitamin C consumption is consistent across social class. There are also regional differences in consumption of vitamin C: as one moves further north within the UK, the consumption gets lower.

However, intakes of retinol and carotene, which have vitamin A activity, are lower among women than men. Vitamin E intakes are also lower because of smaller food intakes and a smaller consumption of vegetables and appropriate vegetable oils. Vitamin E intake also varies with social class: the lower the social class, the lower the vitamin E intake.

In Scotland, where the risk of CHD is the highest in Britain, a surprising number of women do not eat any fresh fruit or green vegetables.[15] Although women tend to eat more fruit than men, and therefore seem to have taken on some of the healthy eating message, in parts of Scotland, some women do not eat green vegetables at all. On average, women in Scotland eat less than two portions of fruit and vegetables a day, and men eat about 1.4 portions.

Low fruit and vegetable consumption may thus be a very important contributor to the high rates of CHD among women in the UK.

Obesity and body fat distribution

Obesity is an important determinant of CHD risk in women. The Royal College of Physicians outlined the risks of obesity in 1983.[16] Although most prospective studies of obesity and CHD have included only men, long-term prospective studies among women show that, as body mass index (BMI) increases, so does the risk of CHD.[1,17,18] Even mild to moderately overweight women have a significantly increased risk of CHD.[1] Many of the effects of obesity are mediated through increases in blood cholesterol, blood pressure and diabetes.

There is a synergistic effect between obesity and other risk factors for CHD, and obesity confers an increased risk of CHD in both the presence and absence of smoking, hypertension, high cholesterol level and diabetes (see Figure 1). The excess risk associated with obesity is particularly high among current smokers and diabetic women.[1]

However, the CHD risk associated with obesity is less than half that associated with cigarette smoking. Smoking, thin women have a far greater risk of death from all causes than obese, non-smoking women. The first priority of any prevention programme or policy must therefore be to address cigarette smoking rather than weight loss. However, dietary advice is also needed when women are counselled to give up smoking since it is important, for both personal and medical reasons, to avoid weight gain thereafter.

There has been a large increase in the proportion of obese women (BMI over 30) in Britain, from 8% in 1980 to 12% in 1986/87. In 1986/87, 36% of women had a BMI over 25, and were thus overweight or obese.[2] By 1992, 16% of women in England were obese, and 45% were overweight or obese.[19] Many women are therefore at increased risk of CHD because of their weight.

FIGURE 1: Effect of interaction of BMI and other CHD risk factors on CHD

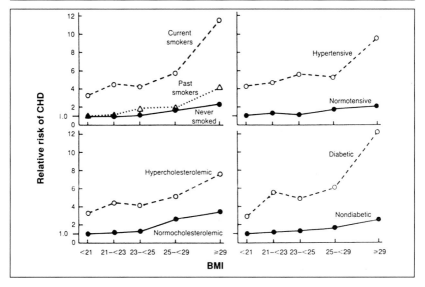

Source: See reference 1.

It is difficult to pinpoint the dietary changes that may have led to the increased prevalence of obesity. However, total fat intake is increasingly recognised to promote the development of obesity in both women and men. Studies suggest that the BMI of adults and children relates to the proportion of energy derived from dietary fat, irrespective of other factors,[13] and that women with high fat diets also have higher BMIs.[20] The higher the fat content of the diet, the greater the average BMI.

Obesity and overweight are a manifestation of the balance of energy intake and expenditure. If a high fat diet tends to promote obesity in an inactive society, then this will become more of a problem in an increasingly inactive society. Inactivity is likely to be one of the major reasons for the increase in obesity (see Chapter 10). This inactivity is now manifest in young children and a clear preventive strategy to maintain a normal body weight, to avoid smoking and to eat a healthy diet, needs to start in childhood if appropriate family habits are to be promoted nationally.

The distribution of fat in the body also appears to be important. A high waist:hip ratio (android distribution) is associated with a much greater risk of myocardial infarction than a low waist:hip ratio (gynoid distribution with thin waist). This applies to the whole range of BMIs. Some studies suggest that the waist:hip ratio may be a better predictor of cardiovascular risk than BMI, among women as well as men.[21] Generally, women tend to have a lower waist:hip ratio than men, although the ratio rises with age.[19]

Conclusion

The cholesterol story is changing. Data compiled over the past 40 years are being re-examined, highlighting the effects of specific fatty acids. This new information has substantial implications for recommendations on diet. However, there will not be sufficient confidence to change dietary recommendations until the Ulbricht and Southgate analyses[5] have been more extensively developed. It is likely to be a long time before the World Health Organization recommends any changes to the figures underlying nutrition policy.

The importance of dietary intervention to reduce the risk of CHD, particularly in post-menopausal women, has been underestimated. Current analyses of poor responses to dietary intervention have been misinterpreted: a failure to reduce serum cholesterol levels by dietary intervention indicates non-compliance and mismanagement, rather than metabolic resistance. This has profound implications for policy: people with high blood cholesterol levels are not 'resistant' to cholesterol-lowering, but are merely resistant to their doctors who may well be providing poor advice.

Women, like men, eat a very high fat diet. The saturated fatty acid content of that diet is improving but the total fat content is not. Fruit and vegetable consumption is remarkably low. Women are making changes in terms of fruit consumption but their vegetable consumption, and therefore their vitamin E consumption, is very low. Women are clearly as susceptible as men in relation to diet and CHD. The problem is how to get women to change their diet. Most of the health education so far has concentrated on men's diets, even though it is the women who are involved in the practical issues of food.

The decline in physical activity with age also leads to a declining food intake, which means that there is a need to have a progressively higher quality or more nutrient-rich diet, in order to maintain antioxidant and mineral intakes.

This section is based on a paper prepared for the National Forum for Coronary Heart Disease Prevention by Professor Philip James, Director of the Rowett Research Institute. Professor James is an individual member of the Forum.

References

1   Manson JE, Colditz GA, Stampfer MJ, Willett WC, Rosner B, Monson RR, Speizer FE, Hennekens CH. 1990. A prospective study of obesity and risk of coronary heart disease in women. *New England Journal of Medicine*; 322: 882-889.

2   Gregory J, Foster K, Tyler H, Wiseman M. Social Survey Division, OPCS. 1990. *The dietary and nutritional survey of British adults.* London: HMSO.

3   Keys A. 1980. *Seven countries: a multivariate analysis of death and coronary heart disease.* London: Harvard University Press.

4   Keys A, Anderson JT, Grande F. 1965. Serum cholesterol response to changes in the diet. I. Iodine value of dietary fat versus 2S-P. *Metabolism*; 14: 747-765.

5   Ulbricht TLV, Southgate DAT. 1991. Coronary heart disease: seven dietary factors. *Lancet*; 338: 985-992.

6   Hegsted DM, McGandy RB, Myers ML, Store FJ. 1965. Quantitative effects of dietary fat on serum cholesterol in man. *American Journal of Clinical Nutrition*; 17: 281-295.

7   Hornstra G, Van Houwelingen AC, Kester ADM, Sundram K. 1991. A palm oil-enriched diet lowers serum lipoprotein (a) in normocholesterolemic volunteers. *Atherosclerosis*; 90: 91-93.

8   Miller GJ, Martin JC, Webster J, Wilkes HC, Miller NE, Wilkinson WH, Meade TW. 1986. Association between dietary fat intake and plasma factor VII coagulant activity – a predictor of cardiovascular mortality. *Atherosclerosis*; 60: 269-277.

9   Hegsted DM. 1991. Dietary fatty acids, serum cholesterol and coronary heart disease. In: *Health effects of dietary fatty acids.* Nelson GJ, ed. Champaign, Illinois: American Oil Chemists Society.

10 Khosla P, Hayes KC. 1992. Comparison between the effects of dietary saturated (16:0), monounsaturated (18:1), and polyunsaturated (18:2) fatty acids on plasma lipoprotein metabolism in cebus and rhesus monkeys fed cholesterol-free diets. *American Journal of Clinical Nutrition*; 55: 51-62.

11 Khosla P, Hayes KC. 1993. Dietary palmitic acid raises plasma LDL cholesterol relative to oleic acid only at a high intake of cholesterol. *Biochimica et Biophysica Acta*; 1210: 13-22.

12 Rouse IL. 1983. Blood pressure lowering effects of a vegetarian diet: controlled trial in normotensive subjects. *Lancet*; 1: 5-9.

13 World Health Organization. 1990. *Diet, nutrition, and the prevention of chronic diseases.* Technical Report Series, 797. Geneva: WHO.

14 Bolton-Smith C, Casey CE, Gey KF, Smith WCS. 1991. Antioxidant vitamin intakes assessed using a food-frequency questionnaire: correlation with biochemical status in smokers and non-smokers. *British Journal of Nutrition*; 65: 337-346.

15 Smith WCS, Tunstall-Pedoe H, Crombie IK, Tavendale R. 1989. Concomitants of excess coronary deaths – major risk factors and lifestyle findings from 10,359 men and women in the Scottish Heart Health Study. *Scottish Medical Journal*; 34: 550-555.

16 Royal College of Physicians. 1983. Obesity. *Journal of the Royal College of Physicians of London*; 17.

17 Hubert HB, Feinleib M, McNamara PM, Castelli WP. 1983. Obesity as an independent risk factor for cardiovascular disease: a 26-year follow-up of participants in the Framingham Heart Study. *Circulation*; 67: 968-977.

18 Lew EA, Garfinkel L. 1979. Variations in mortality by weight among 750,000 men and women. *Journal of Chronic Diseases*; 32: 563-576.

19 Breeze E, Maidment A, Bennett N, Flatley J, Carey S. 1994. *Health survey for England 1992. A survey carried out by the Social Survey Division of OPCS on behalf of the Department of Health.* London: HMSO.

20 George V, Tremblay A, Despres JP, Leblanc C, Bouchard C. 1990. Effect of dietary fat content on total and regional adiposity in men and women. *International Journal of Obesity*; 14: 1085-1094.
21 Lapidus L, Bengtsson C, Larsson B et al. 1984. Distribution of adipose tissue and risk of cardiovascular disease and death: a 12 year follow up of participants in the population study of women in Gothenburg, Sweden. *British Medical Journal*; 289: 1257-1261.

Diet: what are the policy implications for women?

ELIZABETH DOWLER

SUMMARY

Women are often the targets for nutrition policy and intervention, both as consumers and providers, and are important in policy terms.

Women in the UK eat a diet that is high in fat, and have higher intakes of saturated fat as a percentage of energy and a lower P:S ratio (ratio of polyunsaturates to saturates) than men.

Social class differences in diet are complex: those in lower income households eat fewer green vegetables and fresh fruit, and have lower vitamin C intakes, and a diet with a lower P:S ratio compared to those on higher incomes. Among women in the UK, there is a strong inverse relationship between obesity and social class, which is not found in men. Women with a high waist:hip ratio are at particularly high risk of CHD. This may be important for South Asian women.

Most evidence supports the idea that poorer people eat less healthily than others because a healthy diet costs more. A 'healthy' shopping basket costs between 14% and 22% more than an 'unhealthy' basket. Furthermore, it is very difficult to purchase a healthy diet over a long time, in poor circumstances: there is no margin for error.

Policy often assumes that women are the food providers and make all the decisions about food choice and budgeting, but this view is based on earlier research. More information is needed on household decision-making patterns: there are few studies of food choice among women who live alone, in adult-only households, or as lone parents.

Suggestions for future action include: focussing national and local initiatives on poorer women, children and teenagers, and pregnant women; provision of nutritious school meals; and support for local activities such as food co-ops and lunch clubs.

Dietary intakes of particular nutrients have been implicated among the risk factors for coronary heart disease (CHD), although often with little comment on what people actually eat, and why. Obesity, itself a risk factor for CHD, is often equated with 'overeating', and therefore also seen partly as a dietary problem. However, many of these relationships may not be sufficiently clear cut for policy interventions.

Policy on food and nutrition is based on a number of assumptions about how households operate, particularly in relation to food choice and the factors which affect it. There are four main issues to address:

- How do gender and social class affect dietary patterns? Which women should be the focus of concern?
- How is food chosen?
- What is a 'household' in the UK in the 1990s?
- What are the implications for policy?

Which women should be the focus of concern?

Women, particularly those in manual groups, are often the targets for nutrition education and other preventive interventions, both as consumers and as the perceived providers of poor diets. They are therefore very important in policy terms.

Nutrient intakes and dietary patterns vary by occupationally-based social class and indicators of social and economic deprivation. Studies in the UK and Europe[1, 2, 3, 4, 5] show that women in manual occupational classes do not tend to eat the kind of diet recommended for health. The Dietary and Nutritional Survey of British Adults[6] found that women derive 40.3% of food energy from fat – considerably more than the Committee on Medical Aspects of Food Policy (COMA) recommended maximum of 35%. Only 15% of women in the sample met the COMA recommendation. Perhaps more importantly,[7,8] on average, women have higher intakes of saturated fat as a percentage of energy, lower polyunsaturated fat intakes, and a lower P:S ratio (ratio of polyunsaturates to saturates) than men. The P:S ratio is also lower in social classes IV and V than in classes I and II. However, women often eat more fruit, vegetables and salads than men, and are therefore presumed to have higher antioxidant intakes, although vitamin intakes are lower in younger women, and among women in social classes IV and V.[6] The nature of the social class differences in diet is likely to be complex: the Health and Lifestyle Survey, for example, found marked regional differences in the type of diet consumed that could not be entirely explained by social class or smoking habits.[9] Furthermore, Morgan[2] suggests that dietary fat cannot account for changes in social class distribution of CHD mortality.

Occupational social class may be too insensitive an indicator of adult deprivation, especially for women. The Whitehall II study showed strong inverse associations in both women and men, between employment grade and/or car ownership (which are proxy measures for income and social status) and CHD morbidity.[10] Dietary factors were only cursorily investigated, but supported other research findings that poorer people ate fewer 'healthy' foods. In a separate study, Ben-Shlomo and Davey Smith[11] demonstrated a strong correlation between 'deprivation' scores by counties, and mortality from CHD in women and men in England and Wales. They, among others, assert that accumulated health and social deprivation contribute to excess mortality from CHD and other diseases.

Deprivation is a difficult term to define. Although income does not fully explain the problems, it is a useful starting point for understanding purchasing behaviour, and for policy interventions. Evidence indicates that in the UK over the last two decades women have become the main victims of poverty. Women's comparative economic disadvantage occurs in all spheres through which people obtain access to resources: employed women tend to be paid less than men; women do less well than men in terms of access to and levels of state benefits and pensions; and they often experience unequal access to, and control of, resources within the household.[12]

Obesity among women

However obesity is defined, there is a strong, inverse relationship with socioeconomic status among women in the UK, which is not observed in men and young children.[6, 13] In women, this relationship between obesity and socioeconomic status occurs from early adolescence onwards, and is seen in relation to socioeconomic status both of adulthood and of birth. Explanations for this relationship focus on the intense social stigma of obesity in women, and suggest mechanisms whereby women of higher economic status exercise an intellectual, social and economic ability to control their body weight.[14]

Recent evidence suggests that central rather than abdominal obesity is important in the development of CHD and other diseases.[14] A high waist:hip ratio, which is a proxy for intra-abdominal rather than subcutaneous fat, is a strong risk factor for CHD, in both women and men. Women with a high waist:hip ratio are at particularly high risk, not simply those who are overweight or obese. This may be important for the high rates of CHD mortality among South Asian populations, where the usual dietary and other risk factors offer inadequate explanation.

However, fat distribution makes no difference to the ability to lose weight. There is some evidence that individuals with a high waist:hip ratio can reduce their risk by losing weight.

The primary concern should therefore be with poorer women in manual social groups, especially those who are obese and have a high waist:hip ratio.

The effect of nutrition in early childhood

Barker and colleagues have shown a relationship between poor foetal and early child growth, and later mortality from CHD and other causes.[15, 16, 17] Maternal nutritional status, and child care, including infant feeding, are considered critical factors in the interpretation of these observations. Women are likely to be the targets for intervention if this view is accepted, although it is currently controversial. The mechanisms which mediate the familiar inverse relationship between social class and birthweight are not understood.[18] Nonetheless, the women who are important in policy terms are again those who are poorer and/or smaller, as well as those who smoke.

The association between adult height and CHD mortality (short height is linked to higher risk) may provide further evidence of the importance of nutrition in early years and/or adult socioeconomic circumstances.[19]

Using height and weight as indicators of nutritional status
Anthropometric indicators, such as height and weight, have traditionally been used to measure and describe nutritional status. However, the Sub-Committee on Nutrition for the Advisory Coordinating Committee for the United Nations has highlighted the importance of not ascribing causality when using these indicators.[20] Thus, poor child growth, short height and body mass index in adulthood do not necessarily and exclusively denote a nutritional problem or inadequate dietary intakes. Infection, anorexia, and probably general misery, also contribute. However, anthropometry may provide the best general proxy for constraints to human welfare among the poorest groups, including those which cause nutritional deficiency, and environmental health risks.[20]

On the basis of this evidence, then, the women of primary concern are also poorer mothers – or those in social classes IV and V – whose babies are more likely to show poorer foetal development, birthweight and infant growth.

Poverty and diet

Most evidence supports the idea that a healthy diet costs more, certainly in the longer term, and discounts obstinacy or lack of information as reasons for why poorer people eat a less healthy diet.

Figure 1 shows data on expenditure and consumption of different foods from the 1992 National Food Survey,[21] in two income groups. Expenditure on fresh green vegetables and fresh fruit is lower in poorer groups, and this is reflected in consumption. However, the differential in expenditure on bread and potatoes between the two groups is much smaller than the differential in consumption: poorer people eat more of both. It might be concluded that poorer people get better value for money; it might also be concluded they buy cheaper food, which may be of poorer nutritional quality.

FIGURE 1: Consumption and expenditure of food groups in two income groups, 1992

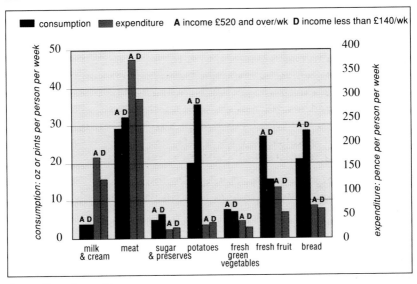

Source: See reference 21.

FIGURE 2: Nutrient intake in two income groups, 1992

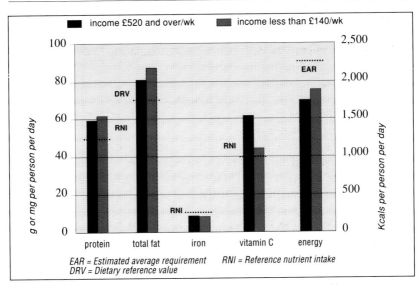

Source: For graph data see reference 21. For EAR/RNI/DRV see reference 22.

Figure 2 indicates the effect of such purchasing patterns on nutrient intake. In particular, vitamin C intakes are low in low income households.[21] Although they are slightly above the reference nutrient intake (RNI) for vitamin C, the UK RNI does not include the high levels thought to be necessary for the prevention of CHD as the Committee on Medical Aspects of Food Policy concluded that the evidence was inconclusive.[22]

Thus, those in the lower income group appear to be better at buying nutrients for any given amount of money, perhaps because they have less to spend. However, in buying cheap calories they also buy more fat.

Data from the National Children's Home Poverty and Nutrition Survey[23] indicate that the average family with children in the UK spends 12.4% of its total expenditure (including housing costs) on food. In contrast, the average family on income support spends 28%, or 43% if housing costs are excluded.

Table 1 shows the cost of 100 calories from snack foods, many of which are commonly eaten by 10-12 year old children. Snack foods may be a sensible option for individuals who are hungry but who do not have much money. Not eating 'healthy' foods may therefore be wise on little money.[23]

TABLE 1: Cost of 100 kcals of various snack foods

	Amount	Cost
Custard cream biscuits	2 biscuits	3p
Sweets	1 small bag	9p
Chocolate bars	$^1/_2$ bar	10p
Crisps	1 bag	12p
Carrots	1lb	20p
Banana	1 medium	20p
Apples	3 small	29p
Oranges	4 small	35p
Celery	2½ heads	£1.44p

Source: See reference 23.

Table 2 shows regional differences in the cost of 'healthy' and 'unhealthy' food baskets. The cost difference between the two baskets is at least 14% in all regions: 21% in rural areas, 19% in inner cities, and 22% in Scotland.[24] Thus poorer people, including poorer women, cannot afford to buy healthy food all the time.

TABLE 2: Regional differences in cost of one week's shopping: 'healthy' and 'unhealthy' food baskets

	'Healthy' basket	'Unhealthy' basket	% difference
Scotland	£36.54	£30.07	22
North East	£32.41	£27.84	17
North West	£31.61	£26.77	18
Midlands	£33.57	£28.25	19
Wales	£35.01	£29.47	14
South East	£35.38	£30.22	16
South West	£33.59	£29.01	16
Rural	£36.46	£30.22	21
Small town	£32.73	£28.44	15
Inner city	£33.19	£27.86	19
Average	£33.49	£28.57	17
n = 43 centres			

Source: See reference 23.

It is sometimes argued that people on low incomes can buy a healthy diet if they purchase wisely. There are several small research and intervention projects underway in the UK to investigate, and suggest improvements in, the purchase and preparation of food on a tight budget.

However, it is very difficult to purchase a healthy diet over a long time, in poor circumstances.[25,26] Just as it is possible to live on state benefit for one week, it is also possible to cost a diet for a week. But this is quite different from operating on very tight margins which do not allow room for individual taste, preferences, choice, and error, or for family members to say 'I don't like this' or 'I want to eat something else today.' There is no margin for error.

How is food chosen?

Little is known about food choice in the UK today. Policy often assumes that households function as rational, cohesive units, and that women make all the decisions about food and budgeting. Such a view may be somewhat naive. Much evidence suggests that households are often places of conflict or, at least, of negotiation between different members operating to their own ends.[12,27]
Food choices and the food budget are two critical areas for negotiation, particularly in low-income households, where they are often a cause of stress.

It is often implicitly assumed that women are the 'providers' for households:

that they buy, store, prepare, serve and generally seem to control the food domain, particularly with regard to children. However, this control may be symbolic rather than real. While women may do much of the food shopping and cooking, this does not necessarily mean that they exercise real power over choice and presentation of food, nor that they are always able to do what they consider best for themselves or other family members.[28] In fact, there is some evidence that in many households men take responsibility for much of the food purchasing and preparation,[29] although observational research is needed to understand what actually happens in practice.

Practices within the family reproduce social divisions and ideologies. It has been pointed out by Charles and Kerr[30] that the food eaten and the way it is eaten are ways in which social relations and divisions are symbolised, reinforced and reproduced on a daily basis. These meanings are socially defined, and change over time, although little is known about the causes of such changes. Indeed, it is difficult to make predictions beyond the general observation that what the middle classes eat today, the working classes will eat tomorrow.[30]

The present possibilities for effective intervention are limited, not least by how little is known of what goes on within households. Most published research on household provision and food choice in the UK is based on observations from the early 1980s, and concentrates on families with children. There are few studies on food choice of women who live alone or in adult-only households (in which most older women will live) or among lone parents (most of whom are women). It is likely, however, that much has changed over the last decade, particularly for richer households. The Economic and Social Research Council set up a new programme of research in 1992, 'The Nation's Diet', to address this area.

Nowadays, individuals tend to snack and 'graze' in eating, often alone, rather than having family meals. More food is purchased from large supermarkets, and more food is eaten outside the home, or as take-away food. Such behaviour affects purchasing patterns, but is also likely to change the social meaning attached to food. Advertisers and the food industry monitor food purchasing behaviour in terms of products and also investigate factors affecting choice.[29] However, such data and conclusions are not often available to social researchers or policy makers, who rely on measuring what people have done, given certain resources and access to supply, rather than finding out what people would like to purchase, and why.

More information is needed on households' decision-making and functioning in the 1990s, in order to influence dietary behaviour. There is a need for better understanding of women's roles in different social classes, age groups, and circumstances, and for better research on the factors affecting food choice. This information would help address the issue of who dietary advice should be aimed at, and which member of the household should be given supplementary income or food, in order to reach those in need.

What is a 'household' in the UK in the 1990s?

A household is not a unique structure. In practice, there are many different household structures and social forms in the UK, showing age, social class and perhaps regional differences. Data from the General Household Survey[31] show that 36% of households are couples with no dependent children, and 27% are one-person households (see Figure 3). Only 24% of households fall into the category of married/cohabiting couple with dependent children (the standard picture of a 'household' in much research and policy); nearly 6% are households with only one adult and dependent children. In fact, one in five of the households with dependent children is headed by a lone parent (this has increased from 8% in 1971), the majority of whom are women. Most of these children therefore also live in economically poorer households: 70% of registered lone-parent households receive Income Support, a means-tested benefit.[32]

Post-menopausal women, a group of concern in terms of CHD, will probably be found mostly in the 'two adults' or 'one-person' households. It would be useful to know how many women over 60 are on low incomes because of low occupational or widow's pensions.

The General Household Survey also gives information on women's economic activity, that is, work for which they are paid outside the home.[31] As Figure 4 shows, the proportion of women who have children and who work has increased over the last decade, although much of this increase has been in part-time work.

FIGURE 3: Household types in Great Britain, 1992

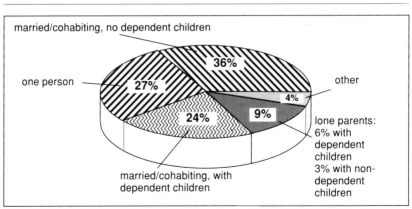

Source: See reference 31.

FIGURE 4: Economic activity of women of working age, with and without dependent children, 1979-92

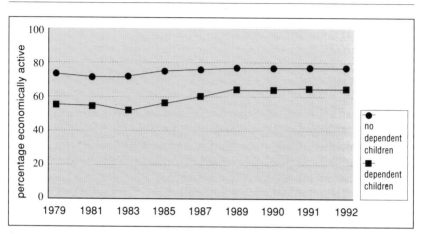

Source: See reference 31.

These figures might suggest that some women now have greater economic independence and therefore, in relation to household provision, more opportunity to express their own food preferences. However, it may well be that women's wages are an essential part of the household budget, and therefore used to buy food and other necessities. Whether women retain control over what they earn is uncertain.

Little contemporary policy in relation to food and nutrition takes account of such household factors explicitly. The Child Support Act (1991) recognises the financial and other problems faced by a society where family structure is increasingly fragile.

What are the implications for policy?

National policy

In the UK, government ideology is that individuals are responsible for their own diets, and for their own health; state responsibility is to enable individuals to make informed food choices.[33] National food policy in the UK has traditionally been devised and implemented by the nutrition sections of the Ministry of Agriculture, Fisheries and Food, and the Department of Health. Nutrition policy has largely been concerned with surveillance, and with influencing choice by nutrition labelling and consumer information, and is often implicitly directed at women as the principal food purchasers. It has had no explicit concern with food entitlement and access. The Health of the Nation Nutrition Task Force in

England, and any Scottish equivalent, have a major role to play in addressing these issues. The primary focus for policy for women should be poorer women and pregnant women. The creation of a Nutrition Task Force Low Income Project Team in 1994 was a welcome step, although the brief does not specifically mention women.

Poorer women

The income of poorer women is clearly an important issue of concern. Effective national nutrition policy intervention for women in general, and poor women in particular, will be difficult unless it addresses the balance between the cost of a healthy diet and the money available for buying food. Pay and employment policy are crucial. Income supplements for families with dependent children are targeted nationally to carers, who are usually women (Child Benefit) and to lone parents (One-Parent Benefit), who tend to be women. The levels of these benefits are low compared with child allowances in the rest of the European Union, and are arguably inadequate to help purchase a healthy diet. Neither has kept pace with inflation over the last decade.

Differential pricing or consumer food subsidies to groups considered to be at nutritional risk are not policy instruments in the UK. The UK does not subsidise food on health grounds, and has reduced the scope of targeted food interventions for specific groups, such as free milk and free school meals.

There is perhaps understandable resistance by the government to raise public expenditure by increasing state benefits to the poor. Nonetheless, it is clear that women in poor households need their own access to more cash, both to improve their own food consumption and to enable them to purchase 'healthy' food for their families.

Foetal development

If foetal development is important in terms of CHD risk, then maternal nutritional status is critical. Nutrition among children and teenagers is particularly important in policy terms, both for their own health and for subsequent pregnancy experience among girls. The provision of nutritious school meals for all school children who want them is an important area for policy.

Pregnant women in lower income groups tend to eat poorer diets than those in professional classes.[34] Furthermore, the Maternity Alliance showed in 1988 that women on means-tested state benefit could not afford to buy a diet that would meet the nutritional requirements for pregnancy set out by the Department of Health.[35]

Maternity provision may also be an important area for policy intervention. The European Directive on Maternity Leave, adopted in 1991, guarantees 14 weeks of paid leave at the level of sick pay prevailing in each member state, and guarantees that a woman cannot be sacked for being pregnant.[36, 37] However, such a guarantee applies only to women in paid employment, and there are various restrictions on entitlement.

Dietary advice

More research is needed on household resource management in different household types. Nutritional or dietary advice should take account of the influences on food choice, and any programme aimed at low income groups has to be realistic and based on current dietary practices and customs.

Local initiatives

There are already many good, local initiatives addressing food and health issues. Many work mainly with women, although they may not be aimed explicitly at them and their specific needs. Such initiatives include support groups, local food co-ops to increase poor families' access to fresh foods, health and dietary information and demonstrations, and lunch clubs, which have been set up by community and self-help groups, community health projects, voluntary organisations, and local authorities and health authorities.[38, 39] Many of these projects seem to succeed because they are seen not to be funded commercially, and so are trusted.[40] However, many are small scale. Funding for such activities has been precarious and is likely to become more so, particularly since local authority and health authority funding is increasingly limited with the introduction of the council tax and changes in the NHS. The National Food Alliance resource pack 'Food and low income' provides examples of local initiatives and guidelines for setting up local projects.[41]

Conclusion

In general, women do take account of health in food choice. They worry a lot about getting or being fat. Many who are poor feel they have little control over their lives and little opportunity to improve their diets. It is important that health and nutrition policy and health education should not merely add to this anxiety and guilt.

Until recently, academic research had little to tell us either about food choice in a contemporary society, or about how to influence it. The food and advertising industry may know much more. Information to consumers is still the principal central policy mechanism; differential pricing is not used much, nor are targeted food interventions.

Household structure, functioning and stability are changing rapidly, and women's traditional role as food providers may also be evolving. Contemporary policy in food and nutrition needs to change to reflect these developments.

This section is based on a paper prepared for the National Forum for Coronary Heart Disease Prevention by Elizabeth Dowler of the Centre for Human Nutrition, Department of Public Health and Policy, London School of Hygiene and Tropical Medicine. A fuller version of this paper has been published in 'Diet and coronary heart disease in women. Potential policy implications'. Dowler E. 1993. Food Policy; June 1993: 224-236.

References

1   Bolton-Smith C, Smith WCS, Woodward M, Tunstall-Pedoe H. 1991. Nutrient intakes in different social class groups: results from the Scottish Heart Health Study. *British Journal of Nutrition*; 65: 321-325.

2   Morgan M, Heller RF, Swerdlow A. 1989. Changes in diet and coronary heart disease mortality among social classes in Great Britain. *Journal of Epidemiology and Community Health*; 43: 162-167

3   Hulshof KFAM, Lowik MRH, Kok FJ, Wedel M, Brants HAM, Hermus RJJ, ten Hoor F. 1991. Diet and other life-style factors in high and low socio-economic groups (Dutch Nutrition Surveillance System). *European Journal of Clinical Nutrition*; 45: 441-450.

4   Rissanen AM, Heliovaara M, Knecht P, Reunanen A, Aromaa A. 1991. Determinants of weight gain and overweight in adult Finns. *European Journal of Clinical Nutrition*; 45: 419-430.

5   Nystrom Peck AM, Vagero DH. 1989. Adult body height, self perceived health and mortality in the Swedish population. *Journal of Epidemiology and Community Health*; 43: 380-384.

6   Gregory J, Foster K, Tyler H, Wiseman M. Social Survey Division, OPCS. 1990. *The dietary and nutritional survey of British adults.* London: HMSO.

7   Ulbricht TLV, Southgate DAT. 1991. Coronary heart disease: seven dietary factors. *Lancet*; 338: 985-992.

8   Crouse JR. 1989. Gender, lipoproteins, diet and cardiovascular risk. *Lancet*; i: 318-320.

9   Whichelow MJ, Erzinclioglu SW, Cox BD. 1991. Some regional variations in dietary patterns in a random sample of British adults. *European Journal of Clinical Nutrition*; 45: 253-262.

10 Marmot MG, Davey Smith G, Stansfield S, Patel C, North F, Head J, White I, Brunner E, Feeney A. 1991. Health inequalities among British civil servants: the Whitehall II study. *Lancet*; 337: 1387-1393.

11 Ben-Shlomo Y, Davey Smith G. 1991. Deprivation in infancy or in adult life: which is more important for mortality risk? *Lancet*; 337: 530-534.

12 Millar J, Glendinning C. 1989. Gender and poverty. *Journal of Social Policy*; 18, no 3: 363-381.

13 Sorbal J, Stunkard AJ. 1989. Socioeconomic status and obesity: a review of the literature. *Psychological Bulletin*; 105, no 2: 260-275.

14 Larsson B. 1991. Obesity, fat distribution and cardiovascular disease. *International Journal of Obesity*; 15: 53-57.

15 Barker DJP, Osmond C. 1986. Infant mortality, childhood nutrition, and ischaemic heart disease in England and Wales. *Lancet*; i: 1077-1081.

16 Barker DJP, Osmond C, Winter PD, Margetts B, Simmonds SJ. 1989. Weight in infancy and death from ischaemic heart disease. *Lancet*; ii: 577-580.

17 Osmond C, Barker DJP, Slattery JM. 1990. Risk of death from cardiovascular disease and chronic bronchitis determined by place of birth in England and Wales. *Journal of Epidemiology and Community Health*; 44: 139-141.

18   Leon D. 1991. Influence of birth weight on differences in infant mortality by social class and legitimacy. *British Medical Journal*; 303: 964-967.

19   Barker DJP, Osmond C, Golding J. 1990. Height and mortality in the counties of England and Wales. *Annals of Human Biology*; 17, no 1: 1-6.

20   Mason JB. 1990. Measuring children: the uses of anthropometry. *SCN News*; no 5: 8-21.

21   Ministry of Agriculture, Fisheries and Food. 1993. *National food survey 1992*. London: HMSO.

22   Department of Health. 1991. *Dietary Reference Values for food energy and nutrients for the United Kingdom. Report of the Panel on Dietary Reference Values of the Committee on Medical Aspects of Food Policy. Report on Health and Social Subjects no 41*. London: HMSO.

23   National Children's Home. 1991. *NCH Poverty and nutrition survey (1991)*. London: National Children's Home.

24   Scottish Office. 1989. *Scottish abstract of statistics*; No 17/1988.

25   Nelson M, Mayer AMB, Manley P. 1992. *Modest-but-adequate budget standards: food budgets for six household types*. Family Budget Unit, University of York.

26   Leather S. 1992. Less money, less choice: poverty and diet in the UK today. In: National Consumer Council (ed). *Your food: whose choice?* London: HMSO.

27   Brannen J, Wilson G (eds). 1987. *Give and take in families: studies in resource distribution*. London: Allen and Unwin.

28   McKie LJ, Wood RC. 1991. Dietary beliefs and practices: a study of working-class women in North East England. *British Food Journal*; 93, no 4: 25-28.

29   Clift C, Fielding D. 1991. *Balance of power: male and female shopping habits*. Lowe Howard-Spink; reported in the *Independent on Sunday*, 27 October, 1991.

30   Charles N, Kerr M. 1988. *Women, food and families*. Manchester: Manchester University Press.

31   Office of Population Censuses and Surveys. 1994. *General household survey 1992*. London: HMSO.

32   Haskey J. 1989. One-parent families and their children in Great Britain: numbers and characteristics. *Population Trends*; 55: 27-33.

33   Wiseman MJ. 1990. Government: where does nutrition policy come from? *Proceedings of the Nutrition Society*; 49, no 3: 397-401.

34   Brooke OG, Anderson HR, Bland JM, Peacock JL, Stewart CM. 1989. Effects on birthweight of smoking, alcohol, caffeine, socioeconomic factors and psychological stress. *British Medical Journal*; 298: 795-801.

35   Durward L. 1988. *Poverty in pregnancy: the cost of an adequate diet for expectant mothers*. London: Maternity Alliance.

36   Commission of European Communities. 1990/91. Maternity leave. *Women of Europe*; 67.

37   Palmer J. 1991. EC compromise on pregnancy pay. *The Guardian*, 7 November.

38   Berry J, Cavill N, King H. 1990. *Take heart: Good practices in coronary heart disease prevention*. London: Health Education Authority.

39   Watson P. 1991. *Community health initiatives and food: an information pack*. London: National Community Health Resource.

40   Garrow JS. 1991. *Obesity and overweight*. London: Health Education Authority.

41   Leather S, Lobstein T. 1994. *Food and low income: a practical guide for advisers and supporters working with families and young people on low income*. London: National Food Alliance.

CHAPTER 9

Hormones

Hormonal influences on women's risk of CHD

JOHN C STEVENSON

SUMMARY
The hormonal changes associated with the menopause seem to add to women's risk of coronary heart disease (CHD). Before the age of menopause, women have relatively low rates of CHD, but after, women's rates become more similar to those of men. The menopause has an adverse effect on blood lipids, including an increase in total cholesterol, LDL cholesterol and triglycerides, and a decrease in HDL cholesterol.

Population studies suggest a reduction in the risk of CHD among post-menopausal women taking oestrogen replacement therapy, and a reduction in mortality among those with existing CHD. However, hormone replacement therapy (HRT) is now usually administered with a progestogen (in combined replacement therapy) and this may have both beneficial and adverse metabolic effects.

Reduced oestrogen levels after the menopause can also lead to adverse changes in hypertension, obesity and body fat distribution, blood clotting factors, glucose metabolism and diabetes, which are important in increasing the incidence of CHD. HRT may reverse some of these changes although certain progestogens may have some unwanted effects. However, long-term prospective studies are needed to assess the overall benefits and risks of different types of HRT and different routes and durations of treatment.

Before the age of the menopause, women have relatively low rates of coronary heart disease (CHD) compared to men. However, at around the time of menopause, the rates become much more similar, and this may be due to the loss of ovarian function and loss of the relative protection. Over the century, female life expectancy has steadily increased, but the age of menopause has not changed. Thus the average woman in the UK can now expect to spend about one-third of her life in the post-menopausal state.

The effects of hormonal changes associated with the menopause are now being seen in increasing numbers in clinical practice. While hormone replacement therapy (HRT) was initially prescribed only for the relief of acute menopausal symptoms (such as hot flushes and vaginal dryness), some clinicians are now prescribing it for the prevention of longer-term ill health, such as osteoporosis and CHD. Discussion about its long-term effects has thus become more important.

Effects of hormones on CHD risk

The menopause seems to have an impact on women's risk of CHD. Data from the Framingham study show an increase in incidence of CHD with increasing age.[1] However, a comparison of age-matched pre-menopausal and post-menopausal women also shows a clear difference between the two groups, suggesting that the menopause itself adds to the risk of developing CHD (see Figure 1).

FIGURE 1: Incidence of cardiovascular disease by menopausal status

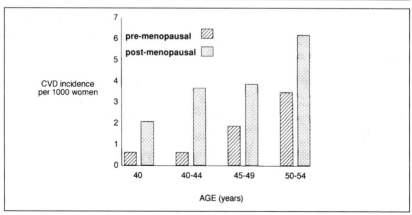

Source: See reference 1.

* ***Throughout this section the abbreviation CRT is used for combined replacement therapy, or opposed therapy, and ORT is used for oestrogen replacement therapy, or unopposed therapy.***

Effects of hormone replacement therapy

Oestrogen replacement therapy (unopposed therapy)

Epidemiological evidence from both prospective and cross-sectional studies suggests that oestrogen replacement therapy (ORT) has an impact on CHD. Population studies suggest a reduction of about 50% in CHD risk among post-menopausal women taking oestrogen replacement therapy.[2] (See also page 143.) Studies from the United States[3] also suggest that, among post-menopausal women with CHD, those who take oestrogens have a much better survival rate than those who do not.

Thus ORT may have benefits for women both in reducing the risk of CHD, and in reducing mortality rates among those with existing CHD.

Combined replacement therapy (opposed therapy)

Almost all the population studies on the effects of HRT have been conducted using oestrogen therapy alone (ORT). However, oestrogen is now usually administered with a progestogen (combined replacement therapy, or CRT). The added progestogen has the effect of reducing the very small, but real, risk of endometrial cancer, and of regulating bleeding patterns in post-menopausal women.

The progestogen addition has both positive and negative metabolic effects,[5] although preliminary evidence suggests that the addition of progestogen may not necessarily negate the beneficial effects of oestrogen on the incidence of CHD.

Effect of hormones on blood lipids

Average blood cholesterol levels in the UK increase with age, throughout adult life. However, there also seems to be an additional increase in total cholesterol levels in women due to the menopause. Figure 2 shows cholesterol levels in 542 healthy women, divided into pre-menopausal and post-menopausal women by hormonal assessment.

FIGURE 2: Effect of ageing and menopause on cholesterol levels

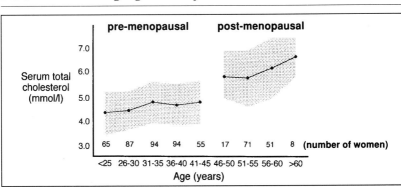

Source: See reference 4.

However, total cholesterol is a fairly crude index for examining lipid abnormalities. Following the menopause there are also increases in LDL cholesterol and triglycerides, and decreases in some HDL cholesterol subfractions,[4] an adverse lipid pattern which is likely to be associated with increased risk of CHD.

Oestrogen replacement therapy (ORT) reverses some of these changes. The main effects of oestrogen on lipoproteins include: a reduction in total and LDL cholesterol, a small increase in both HDL cholesterol and the more important HDL_2 subfraction, and, unfortunately, an increase in triglycerides (with oral oestrogen administration). It is possible that triglycerides may be an independent risk factor for women, and the overall effect (benefit or risk) is therefore uncertain. Whether oestrogens affect 'newer' lipid risk factors, such as $lipoprotein_a$ (Lp_a), has still to be seen.

Added progestogen does not affect the LDL cholesterol-lowering effect of oestrogen, but may reverse the HDL-raising effect. The increase in HDL cholesterol brought about with oestrogen alone in the usual doses is relatively minor. Added progestogen may either reverse this by producing a very small fall in HDL cholesterol or may have no effect. This may be of concern, if it is oestrogen's HDL cholesterol-raising effect in post-menopausal women that reduces the risk of future CHD. Progestogen also reduces triglyceride level, but also has the possible adverse effect of increasing insulin resistance.

However, it is important to bear in mind that different types of progestogen have different effects, and the metabolic impact depends on the type of progestogen. These results are seen with the older, more potent progestogens; the newer progestogens may have less metabolic impact.

There is therefore a conflict with added progestogens in combined replacement therapy (CRT), as some of the effects are beneficial, and others seem to be potentially more adverse.

Impact of different rates of administration of HRT

There are different routes of administering HRT including skin patches, oral administration, and subcutaneous implants and it is possible that these different routes have different effects on blood lipids.[6] This may be important in terms of tailoring therapy to have the best effect. Figure 3 shows the effects of the different routes of administration of HRT on lipid levels. It compares the effects of HRT, both oestrogen replacement therapy (E) and combined replacement therapy (EP) on total cholesterol and on triglycerides, when administered orally or transdermally, over a six-month study period.[6] During the third month women were studied taking no HRT, or oestrogen only (E), or oestrogen plus progestogen (EP); during the sixth month women were studied taking either no HRT or oestrogen plus progestogen (EP). The significance of changes among women taking HRT is measured against women not taking HRT.

FIGURE 3: Impact of different routes of administration of HRT on lipid levels

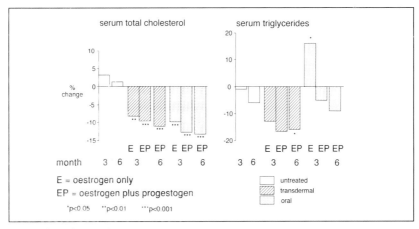

Source: See reference 6.

In terms of risk factors for CHD, there is little research on subcutaneous oestrogen implants. However, it is clear from results on other non-oral routes that implants are likely to have a similar effect to the oestrogen skin patches, although implants produce a much higher oestradiol level in the blood, which may indeed sometimes be too high. Too much hormone can be as bad as too little hormone. There is a need for more data on implant therapy, although at present its use is confined to a small number of centres.

Effect of hormones on other CHD risk factors

Processes involved in the development of CHD may be either beneficially or adversely affected by HRT. Much of the emphasis so far has been on lipids. However, a whole series of interrelated factors are important in increasing the incidence of CHD, including risk factors such as hypertension, obesity, lipids, blood-clotting factors, glucose metabolism and diabetes. Reaven[7] has proposed that these risk factors may be centrally linked through the resistance of the body's tissues to the action of insulin. Increasing insulin levels may therefore cause damage both on their own and through these other pathways.

Carbohydrate metabolism and insulin secretion
HRT has various effects on carbohydrate metabolism. A study of 90 post-menopausal women showed an impairment of the glucose response among those taking oral HRT, which was not seen in those with transdermal skin treatment.[8]

This could be due either to the different route of administration or to the different types of oestrogen and progestogen used.

Reduced oestrogen levels following the menopause seem to lead to a reduction in the secretion of insulin, which may be reversed by HRT. However, there are differences in insulin resistance or sensitivity among women taking oestrogen alone compared to those taking oestrogen and progestogen, when administered orally: the progestogen has a particularly adverse effect, which needs to be addressed.

Obesity and body fat distribution

Obesity and the distribution of body fat are also important in the development of CHD.The body mass index (BMI, or weight/height^2), commonly used in population studies, provides information on the amount of body fat, but not its location. The distribution of fat in the body can be separated into two types: central, android, classical male distribution of fat, or classical female, gynoid distribution around the hips and thighs. Android distribution is associated with a higher risk of CHD, and this distinction may be as, if not more, important than the total amount of fat. The measurement of fat distribution can be quick and non-invasive.[9]

The distribution of fat can be related to other metabolic abnormalities, such as the ratio of HDL cholesterol to LDL cholesterol. A lower ratio is more atherogenic. An increase in the proportion of fat in the android distribution correlates well with a reduction in the ratio of HDL cholesterol to LDL cholesterol. Similarly, insulin resistance increases as fat distribution becomes more android.

The distribution of body fat in women is influenced by hormonal factors. In pre-menopausal women, the distribution of body fat is very different to that of men. In post-menopausal women, however, the distribution becomes more android.[9] HRT leads to a reduction in the amount of fat in the android distribution.

Blood clotting processes

Very little is known about the effects of hormones on the processes which form or dissolve blood clots (thrombosis and fibrinolysis). However, levels of fibrinogen and Factor VII, both of which promote blood clotting, increase after the menopause, and HRT increases the level of antithrombin III, which prevents blood clotting.[10] The different routes of administration of HRT may have different effects, and these also need to be taken into consideration. Further research is needed in order to understand the full effects of HRT on blood clotting.

Changes in blood vessels

HRT may also directly affect the development of CHD through changes in the blood vessels. Average blood pressure levels in UK women increase with age. In general there is a small decrease in blood pressure in women taking HRT.

Studies[11] have found that arterial resistance to blood flow increases over time after the menopause. With HRT, this increase in resistance is reversed. The presence of oestradiol receptors throughout the human arterial tree suggests that oestrogen may have a direct effect on the arterial walls, either through an endothelium-dependent mechanism[12] or through calcium-dependent mechanisms.[13] Clinical studies have also shown that post-menopausal women with angina due to atherosclerosis improve their ischaemia and their total exercise time during ECG exercise testing, in response to the acute administration of oestrogen.[14]

Conclusion

The reduction in hormone levels associated with menopause produces changes which are in keeping with an increase in the risk of CHD. HRT seems to produce metabolic changes that are in a beneficial direction and therefore may explain, at least in part, the reduction in CHD risk.

However, many questions concerning the clinical management of post-menopausal women remain unanswered. For example:

- How do you identify which post-menopausal women are at greatest risk of CHD?
- What type of oestrogen should be used?
- Which dose gives the best effects on CHD risk?
- What is the impact of added progestogen, and which is the best progestogen?
- What is the impact of different routes of administration of HRT?
- How long must the treatment be continued in order to benefit the cardiovascular system?
- Is the type and dose of HRT prescribed by an individual clinician actually doing any good?

Although most of the above questions could be answered in relation to osteoporosis, they remain unanswered for CHD.

The different oestrogens, progestogens and routes of administration need to be examined, to assess the different metabolic effects and to find the combination that gives the most overall benefit. Long-term prospective studies should then be carried out using those preparations to assess their benefits and risks.

This section is based on a paper prepared for the National Forum for Coronary Heart Disease Prevention by Dr John C Stevenson, Director, Wynn Institute for Metabolic Research and Honorary Senior Lecturer, National Heart and Lung Institute.

References

1   Gordon T, Kannel WB, Hjortland MC, McNamara PM. 1978. Menopause and coronary heart disease. The Framingham Study. *Annals of Internal Medicine*; 89: 157-161.
2   Knopp RH. 1988. The effects of postmenopausal estrogen therapy on the incidence of arteriosclerotic vascular disease. *Obstetrics and Gynecology*; 72: 23S-30S.
3   Sullivan JM, Zwang RV, Hughes JP et al. 1990. Oestrogen replacement and coronary artery disease. *Archives of Internal Medicine*; 150: 2557-2562.
4   Stevenson JC, Crook D, Godsland IF. 1993. Influence of age and menopause on serum lipids and lipoproteins in healthy women. *Atherosclerosis*; 98: 83-90.
5   Crook D, Stevenson JC. 1991. Progestogens, lipid metabolism and hormone replacement therapy. *British Journal of Obstetrics and Gynaecology*; 98: 749-750.
6   Crook D, Cust MP, Gangar KF, Worthington M, Hillard TC, Stevenson JC, Whitehead MI, Wynn V. 1992. Comparison of transdermal and oral estrogen/progestin hormone replacement therapy: effects on serum lipids and lipoproteins. *American Journal of Obstetrics and Gynecology*; 166: 950-955.
7   Reaven GM. 1988. Role of insulin resistance in human disease. *Diabetes*; 37: 1595-1607.
8   Godsland IF, Gangar K, Walton C, Cust MP, Whitehead MI, Wynn V, Stevenson JC. 1993. Insulin resistance, secretion and elimination in post-menopausal women receiving oral or transdermal hormone replacement therapy. *Metabolism*; 42; 7: 846-853.
9   Ley CJ, Lees B, Stevenson JC. 1992. Sex- and menopause-associated changes in body-fat distribution. *American Journal of Clinical Nutrition*; 55: 950-954.
10 Meade TW. 1990. Oestrogens and thrombosis. In: Drife JO, Studd JWW (eds). *HRT and osteoporosis*. London: Springer-Verlag: 223-233.
11 Gangar KF, Vyas S, Whitehead M, Crook D, Meire H, Campbell S. 1991. Pulsatility index in internal carotid artery in relation to transdermal oestradiol and time since menopause. *Lancet*; 388: 839-842.
12 Williams JK, Adams MR, Klopfenstein HS. 1990. Estrogen modulates responses of atherosclerotic coronary arteries. *Circulation Research*; 81: 1680-1687.
13 Collins P, Rosano GMC, Jiang C, Lindsay D, Sarrel PM, Poole-Wilson PA. 1993. Cardiovascular protection by oestrogen – a calcium antagonist effect? *Lancet*; 341: 1264-1265.
14 Rosano GMC, Sarrel PM, Poole-Wilson PA, Collins P. 1993. Beneficial effect of oestrogen on exercise-induced myocardial ischaemia in women with coronary artery disease. *Lancet*; 342: 133-136.

The policy implications of HRT: is there a case for preventive intervention?

KLIM MCPHERSON

SUMMARY
There is evidence that oestrogen replacement therapy may be protective against coronary heart disease (CHD). Newer HRT formulations include progestogen, which may reduce this apparent benefit, but there is a lack of epidemiological data on the long-term effects of the new formulations. Also, many of the apparent effects on CHD may be due to selection bias or compliance bias. One of the most important consequences of HRT may be an increase in the risk of breast cancer. This issue needs to be addressed when evaluating the policy implications of HRT.

The question for policy makers is 'Should HRT be prescribed with the aim of preventing CHD?' Cost benefit analysis shows that HRT is a relatively expensive intervention for CHD prevention.

Individual women will evaluate the short and long-term benefits and risks of HRT in different ways. Since the epidemiology is currently uncertain, it is important that women are fully informed of the uncertainties to make their own decisions.

There has been a rapid increase in use of HRT in the UK, a trend which is likely to continue with vigorous promotion of HRT by drug companies. Before HRT is widely prescribed for reducing the risk of CHD, the policy and cost implications need to be addressed.

The issues of benefit and risk are not resolved and there is a need for clinical trial data on HRT. In the meantime, the emphasis in primary prevention of CHD should be on a long-term population approach rather than mass medication of large numbers of women before the evidence is complete.

Hormone replacement therapy (HRT) clearly offers women relief from menopausal symptoms and reduces the risk of osteoporosis and subsequent fractures. There is also evidence that it may be protective against coronary heart disease (CHD). However, the benefits are not achieved entirely without cost: perhaps the most obvious cost of taking oestrogen replacement therapy (ORT*) for menopausal symptoms is the increased risk of endometrial cancer.

Before HRT is widely prescribed to reduce the risk of CHD among women, the policy implications, and in particular the cost implications of such therapy, need to be properly considered by policy makers and practitioners. Are the benefits sufficient to justify the costs of the prophylactic use of HRT?

Effects of different types of HRT on disease risk

Over recent years, there has been a change in the type of HRT that is widely used, and combined replacement therapy (CRT*) – oestrogen therapy with added progestogen – is now more common. Progestogen is added in order to reduce or eliminate the extra risk of endometrial cancer associated with ORT.

Although the short-term consequences of this change in formulation may be reasonably well understood, the long-term effects on the risk of disease are quite poorly understood. The relatively recent change in practice and prescription makes epidemiological research more difficult. The epidemiology has been dominated by the preponderance – particularly in the United States – of ORT. Most of the research was carried out on the kind of preparations that women are no longer taking, and thus the effects of CRT are quite uncertain. Ten or 20 years' follow-up are needed in order to assess the impact of the newer formulations on chronic diseases such as breast cancer or CHD. The interpretation of the data is therefore compromised by that uncertainty.

Coronary heart disease and stroke
Over 30 epidemiological studies have evaluated the effect of oestrogen replacement use on cardiovascular disease, since 1970. Almost all of these studies are based on the use of unopposed oestrogen, and are observational. They suggest a substantial reduction in CHD risk among women using oestrogen, although the size of the effect, and the explanations, are under debate.[1, 2]

One quantitative overview of the epidemiological literature, including 16 prospective studies, showed an overall relative risk of 0.56 associated with oestrogen use,[3] a figure supported by other meta-analyses. Fifteen of the studies showed decreased relative risks, mostly statistically significant. One of the largest of these studies[4] examining the cardiovascular effects of ORT followed up 48,000 women for 10 years. It reported a 40% reduction in the risk of CHD

---

* Throughout this section the abbreviation ORT is used for oestrogen replacement therapy, or unopposed therapy, and CRT is used for combined replacement therapy, or opposed therapy.

for current oestrogen users. It also indicated a reduction of 20% for former users, although the duration of effect after cessation of treatment is inconclusive. There was no effect on stroke.[4] Evidence for any protective effect of oestrogen on the risk of stroke is diminishing.[4,5]

It is uncertain whether CRT reduces the risk of CHD to the same extent as ORT and what its effect on stroke is. One large prospective cohort study following up over 23,000 women in Sweden,[6] among others, provides epidemiological evidence for the possibility of a differential effect associated with CRT compared to ORT.

There is a lack of data on the effects of CRT on CHD. Since most progestogens adversely affect blood lipid profiles, it is possible that the 'cardioprotective' effect of the older ORT is entirely attenuated by the addition of progestogen. However, different progestogens have different effects and there is some hope that low doses of the androgenic progestogens, and the newer non-androgenic progestogens will avoid this.[7]

Almost all the data on the long-term benefits and risks of HRT are based on observational data and therefore, many of the apparent 'cardioprotective' effects of HRT may be attributable to some kind of selection bias (for example, doctors tend to prescribe HRT to healthier women in higher social classes); and to compliance bias (for example, randomised double-blind clinical trials show that people who comply with placebo treatment get as much cardiovascular benefit as those who comply with active drug treatment.[2,8,9]) Thus it is unclear whether the drug itself has the effects, or whether the type of women who take the drug are intrinsically less likely to get CHD.

Breast cancer*

The effect of HRT on subsequent risk of breast cancer is of major importance both to individual women, and in any analysis of the policy implications of giving HRT as a preventive measure.

Breast cancer incidence rates in women in the UK rise rapidly with age until the menopause, when the rate of increase begins to slow down. This slowing down, which contrasts with CHD rates at this age, is likely to be hormonally

---

* The two speakers whose papers form this chapter disagreed on the long-term health impact of HRT on breast cancer. Professor McPherson argued that the epidemiology and the biology quite conclusively indicate that taking HRT over a long period of time increases the risk of breast cancer. Dr Stevenson argued that the epidemiological evidence that HRT reduces the incidence of CHD is more convincing than the evidence of any increase in risk of breast cancer associated with HRT. He reported that the Bergkvist study, which is often quoted as showing an increase in the diagnosis of breast cancer with HRT, also revealed that women with breast cancer who were taking HRT had lower mortality rates than those who were not taking it.[10,13] He suggested that it is hard to understand how this could occur, unless there are other biases in the study, which would question the validity of the whole study.[21] Bergkvist et al, however, have pointed out that there are many possible confounding factors that need to be taken into account before a direct effect of oestrogen on survival can be attributed.[10]

induced. Many epidemiological studies have shown that women with a naturally delayed menopause have an increased risk of breast cancer, and women with an early menopause (particularly if surgically induced by removal of both ovaries) have a reduced incidence.[11]

One of the consequences of ORT is a continued rise in the incidence of breast cancer: the incidence rate does not slow down as it would with natural menopause. Results of a meta-analysis of 16 studies[12] summarising data on the effect of long-term ORT suggest a 30% increase in risk of breast cancer following 15 years' use (relative risk = 1.3). Among women who started ORT pre-menopausally, the relative risk is about 2. If only European studies are included, the relative risk of breast cancer is 2.5. The risk is particularly high in women with a family history of breast cancer. One large study examining the impact of duration of HRT on the incidence of breast cancer found a relative risk of about 1.7 associated with nine or more years' use.[13]

The effect of added progestogen on breast cancer is currently unknown, but the small amount of research that has been carried out suggests that it may compound the risk.[13, 14]

Thus, at present, the epidemiology points to an increase in the risk of breast cancer after 10 years on CRT, which may be of the order of 25% to 50%.[12] Such an effect, if real, is slightly less than a natural delay in the menopause would predict. This may be compensated for by any benefits on cardiovascular disease, but the cost-benefit equation is therefore finely balanced.

The impact of HRT on breast cancer rates is one of the major issues that has to be addressed in evaluating the policy implications of using HRT as a preventive measure.[14]

Overall mortality

Epidemiological data from the United States among post-menopausal women shows that overall survival is 20% higher among those taking ORT than among women not taking it. In the Nurses' Health Study,[4] for example, the all-cause mortality was 0.89 for ORT users.

Cost-benefit analysis of the preventive use of HRT

We (see reference 15) have analysed data on the benefits, risks and costs of HRT (both CRT and ORT) in the menopause in order to examine the extent to which HRT may be used as a prophylaxis against CHD. The analysis used imaginary cohorts of women, some of whom took HRT and some of whom did not.

Epidemiological conclusions on the relative risks of different diseases were applied to the two cohorts. Epidemiological evidence indicates that, in women who take HRT from age 50 to age 60, there is no increased risk of breast cancer for the first 10 years, but there is a 30% excess in risk over the following 10 years. The relative risk then returns, at age 70, to 1. For CHD, the assumption is that the effect of CRT will be less than the effect of ORT. This leads to a 10% reduction in risk of CHD at age 55-59, and a 30% reduction at age 60-64. For stroke, there appears to be a rather small reduction of risk of about 10%. The effects of ORT on the incidence of CHD and stroke are greater. However, massive reductions are seen in the incidence of fracture (see Table 1).

TABLE 1: Standard risk assumptions (relative risk) for 10 years' HRT from age 50 years

	AGE (years)				
	50-54	**55-59**	**60-64**	**65-69**	**70+**
Assumptions for combined HRT (CRT)					
Breast cancer	1	1	1.3	1.3	1
Ischaemic heart disease	1	0.9	0.7	0.9	1
Cardiovascular disease	1	0.9	0.9	0.9	1
Fracture	0.8	0.4	0.4	0.8	1
Assumptions for oestrogen therapy (ORT)					
Breast cancer	1	1	1.3	1.3	1
Ischaemic heart disease	1	0.7	0.5	0.7	1
Cardiovascular disease	1	0.9	0.7	0.9	1
Fracture	0.8	0.4	0.4	0.8	1

Source: See reference 15.

Table 2 shows hospital admissions (to age 69) attributable to 10 years on HRT, from age 50, comparing 1,000 women not taking HRT with an equal number on CRT. The 'Control' column shows the number of admissions that would be expected in a cohort of 1,000 women not taking any HRT. The 'CRT' column adds the relative risk assumptions associated with CRT usage, which leads to more admissions for some causes such as breast cancer, and fewer admissions for others, including CHD. The increase in hysterectomy and dilation and curettage rates (D & C) are a probable consequence of the monitoring and investigation in women taking the drugs. Overall, the percentage increase in hospital admissions is 1%.

TABLE 2: Hospital admissions attributable to 10 years' CRT use among 50-69 year old women

		+ = *hospital admissions induced*
		− = *hospital admissions prevented*
Admissions for:	**Control** (n=1,000)	**CRT** (n=1,000)
Breast cancer	72	+11
Endometrial cancer	20	no change
Fractured hip	19	-7
Ischaemic heart disease	91	-12
Cardiovascular disease	49	-4
Hysterectomy	54	+9
Dilation and curettage	136	+21
Other causes	1,634	+4
Total	**2,075**	**+22**

Source: See reference 15.

Table 3 shows a simple discounted life year analysis measuring the total cost associated with two sets of assumptions about the effect of oestrogen on cardiovascular risk when it is administered with progestogen in CRT. It assesses the average years of life gained, and the costs, as a consequence of giving women CRT. In the central column, it is assumed that the cardiovascular benefits of oestrogen are halved by the addition of a progestogen. The cost per discounted life year gained under this conservative risk assumption is £14,400. Column 3 assumes, more optimistically, that CRT has the same cardiovascular benefits as ORT: that is, the benefits are not reduced by the addition of progestogen. It applies the relative risks of CHD and stroke in women who take ORT. The cost per discounted life year gained under this assumption would be £7,000.

This means that the cost/benefit ratio of prophylactic use of CRT can be placed in the context of other ways that money can be spent in the health service. Both £14,400 and £7,000 are expensive costs per discounted life year.

The costs are essentially health service costs: hospital and drugs costs associated with admissions, consultations and prescriptions. They do not include costs to the community and to individual women. Thus the cost of a stroke is far higher than the cost of breast cancer on such a scale.

A comparison of different durations of HRT administration shows that for all periods, HRT is an expensive intervention, although the cost per life year reduces over time.[15] Over five years of CRT use, the cost per discounted life year is £31,400. Over 10 years, it is £14,400, and over 15 years, it decreases to £10,400.

TABLE 3: Average life years gained and costs per life year gained for 10 years' CRT, assuming different cardiovascular benefits

	Combined HRT (CRT) *Reduced cardiovascular benefit*	Combined HRT (CRT) *Full cardiovascular benefit**
Total cost per user	£482	£492
Average life years gained per user	0.11	0.24
Cost per discounted life year gained	£14,400	£7,000

* Assumes that the addition of progestogen does not reduce the cardiovascular benefits of oestrogen.

Source: See reference 15.

Sensitivity analysis

A sensitivity analysis gives an assessment of the consequences of the different assumptions made in calculating costs. Table 4 illustrates the consequences of different relative risks of breast cancer associated with 10 years' use of CRT. If CRT had no effect on the risk of breast cancer, the cost per discounted life year would be £10,200. However, as the estimated risk of breast cancer increases, both in magnitude and duration, the cost per discounted life year gained also increases. For example, if the relative risk of breast cancer is, as assumed, 1.3 between ages 60 and 70, and then decreases back to 1 after age 70, the cost is £14,400 per discounted life year. However, if the relative risk of 1.3 persists after age 70, the cost increases to £19,100. A two-fold increase in breast cancer (relative risk of 2) prevailing for 10 years or more, which is not implausible,

TABLE 4: Cost per discounted life year gained after 10 years' use of CRT, assuming different relative risks of breast cancer

	AGE						
	50-54	55-59	60-64	65-69	70+	Life years gained	Cost per discounted life year gained
Estimated relative risk of breast cancer	1	1	2	2	2	-0.20	–
	1	1	2	2	1	-0.01	–
	1	1	1.3	1.3	1.3	0.06	£19,100
	1	1	1.3	1.3	1	0.11	£14,400
	1	1	1	1	1	0.17	£10,200

Source: See reference 15.

would lead to a reduction in overall life expectancy: the excess mortality from breast cancer would wipe out all benefits in relation to cardiovascular disease. The cost per discounted life year than becomes incalculable: life would actually be being lost as a consequence of spending this money on 'prevention'.

Thus, if the risk of breast cancer with CRT turns out to be higher and the cardiovascular risks less, the case for preventive use of HRT is entirely lost. Such a state of affairs would lead to an overall decrease in life expectancy, even taking into account the effect on osteoporosis. In view of current epidemiological evidence, this level of relative risk does not seem to be implausible. Great care is therefore required in policy formation.

Policy implications

The question for policy makers and health professionals is: 'Should women be prescribed HRT with the aim of preventing CHD?' The relative costs of different interventions per quality adjusted life year (QALY) have been calculated. For 10 years of CRT, for a woman aged 50 with mild menopausal symptoms, the cost in 1991 was £6,200 per quality adjusted life year gained: only slightly less than that for heart transplantation, and slightly more expensive than breast cancer screening.[15] CRT is therefore on the margin of cost-effective interventions. Even for treating women who have had a hysterectomy, and therefore highly effective ORT, the cost for preventive use alone is not cheap relative to the benefit.

However, QALYs are based on the assumptions made about benefits and risks and on subjective judgements about quality of life. For HRT, they will depend on the relative weight women give to menopausal symptoms as well as assumptions about long-term benefits and risks in terms of CHD and other diseases.[16,17]

The total programme costs for England and Wales can be calculated by applying these costs to the actual population. By the age of 50, some 18% of women will have had a hysterectomy, and therefore could take ORT, and the remaining 82% would be given CRT. With full compliance, the programme cost would be £121 million over one year (1991 figures). Assuming a less optimistic compliance of 67% for the first five years, and 33% for the following five years, the total programme cost would be about £66 million a year.

However, there are also social class differences in the use of HRT: it is middle-class women at lower risk of CHD who are most likely to take it. The cost-benefit equations would clearly change if HRT was given to individuals at higher risk. However, on the basis of current epidemiology, it seems unlikely that it would make a cost-beneficial intervention even among women at particularly high risk of CHD.

In the end, however, the decision must be made by the individual woman, fully advised about the current epidemiology, and taking into account personal symptoms and preferences. Individual women will value the interventions and their short and long-term risks and benefits in different ways, trading off breakthrough bleeding, breast cancer and CHD, osteoporosis and the other effects of HRT. A trade-off approach could be used to examine the extent to which women in different situations would trade a slightly lower risk of dying of CHD in the long term against a probable increase in the risk of breast cancer. The fear of breast cancer may well reduce the acceptability of HRT. For a woman, the quality of life will also be important: epidemiological analyses are often too crude in assessing only life years gained.

Since the epidemiology is currently uncertain and does not predict an unambiguous cost-effective gain, it is crucial that women are properly informed of the various risks, as they are currently understood, and are given the choice on the basis of their symptoms and their preferences.

However, the issue of mass prescription of HRT, in the direction seen in the United States, needs to be fully discussed and addressed by policy makers. There has been a rapid increase in the use of HRT over the past decade, which has accelerated in the early 1990s. Snapshot surveys indicate that in 1990, 9% of women aged 45 to 59 were current users of HRT and by 1993, this had doubled to 18%.[18, 19] In the UK at present, women tend to take HRT for relatively short periods of time, but it is possible that with the vigorous promotion and marketing by drug companies, attitudes may change and the UK could become more like the United States, where women now take HRT for up to 30 years. At the current rate of increase, over a third of women over 50 could potentially be taking HRT by the year 2000.

HRT shows parallels with cholesterol-lowering treatment, in terms of its enormous resource and cost implications. The potential users, and also the health professionals who write the prescriptions, need proper information in order to offer a considered opinion.

The issues of risk and benefit are not yet resolved. The current controversy about HRT mirrors the problems of oral contraceptives discussed almost 15 years ago.[20] Many different oestrogens and progestogens are available, with different costs and different effects. It is increasingly clear that the effect of HRT on the risk of CHD depends on the type of progestogen that is added. These different types of HRT can also be administered via several routes, in varying doses, using continuous or cyclic schedules, and this will also have an impact on the health effects.

The basic scientific knowledge, both about the physiological and metabolic effects of HRT and about the different combinations of oestrogens and progestogens, is insufficient to make fully informed choices. The pharmacological effects of the preparations are not fully understood, and research is inconclusive in terms of the consequences on disease. It is impossible to extrapolate from one drug to understand the effects of another. Furthermore, there are large differences in the way that individual women metabolise the same hormone.

The combined oral contraceptive pill was prescribed for many years in a vacuum of knowledge among those who were prescribing it. This may still be the case, both for oral contraceptives, and for HRT. Much more research on the newer preparations is needed, before informed choices can be made.

Policy should focus on preventing CHD in known and effective ways, and the other health implications of any intervention must be included in the equation. Both the epidemiology and the biology point quite conclusively to the fact that taking HRT over a long period of time increases the risk of breast cancer. The impact of such a hormone-induced risk on the large number of older women in the UK could be enormous.

Primary prevention programmes for CHD are feasible, and the emphasis should be on a long-term population approach rather than mass medication of a large number of women before the evidence is complete. The focus should be on the achievable rather than the uncertain.

Furthermore, hormonal factors are only one of the factors which influence the risk of CHD. Women in Japan have the lowest rates of CHD in the world, but also low oestrogen levels. Even if a woman takes HRT, she is most likely to die of heart attack or stroke. HRT does not prevent CHD entirely, but may merely reduce the risk of premature disease.

Conclusion

Epidemiology does not give unambiguous answers, and there are many problems with interpretation of the studies on HRT. Almost all of the data on the long-term benefits and risks of HRT are based on observational data, so many of the apparent 'cardioprotective' effects of HRT may be attributable to some kind of selection bias or compliance bias.

There is a lack of clinical trial data and a need for a randomised controlled prospective trial to quantify the overall long-term benefits and risks associated with the prolonged use of current formulations of HRT, before it is used as a preventive measure.

In the meantime, policy should focus on reducing the risk of CHD among women in known and effective ways and on proper discussion of the available evidence on HRT. Health professionals should ensure that women are able to make choices with full information on the uncertainties and on the risks, as well as the potential benefits of HRT.

This section is based on a paper prepared for the National Forum for Coronary Heart Disease Prevention by Professor Klim McPherson, Head of the Health Promotion Sciences Unit, London School of Hygiene and Tropical Medicine. Professor McPherson is an individual member of the Forum.

An updated cost-benefit analysis can be found in 'Hormone replacement therapy in a risk-benefit perspective'. Daly E, Vessey MP, Barlow D, Gray A, McPherson K, Roche M. 1993. Proceedings of the 7th International Congress on the Menopause (Stockholm).

References

1   Barrett-Connor E, Bush TL. 1991. Estrogen and coronary heart disease in women. *Journal of the American Medical Association*; 265: 1861-1867.
2   Petitti DB. 1994. Coronary heart disease and estrogen replacement therapy. Can compliance bias explain the results of observational studies? *Annals of Epidemiology*; 4: 115-118.
3   Stampfer MJ, Colditz GA. 1991. Estrogen replacement therapy and coronary heart disease: a quantitative assessment of the epidemiologic evidence. *Preventive Medicine*; 20: 47-63.
4   Stampfer MJ, Colditz GA, Willett WC, Manson JE, Rosner B, Speizer FE, Hennekens CH. 1991. Postmenopausal estrogen therapy and cardiovascular disease: ten-year follow-up from the Nurses' Health Study. *New England Journal of Medicine*; 325: 756-762.
5   Grady D, Rubin SM, Petitti DB, Fox CS, Black D, Ettinger B, Ernster VL, Cummings SR. 1992. Hormone therapy to prevent disease and prolong life in postmenopausal women. *Annals of Internal Medicine*; 117: 1016-1037.
6   Falkeborn M, Persson I, Adami H-O et al. 1992. The risk of acute myocardial infarction after oestrogen and oestrogen-progestogen replacement. *British Journal of Obstetrics and Gynaecology*; 99; 10: 821-828.
7   Tepper R, Goldberger S, May JY, Jair Luz I, Beyth Y. 1992. Hormonal relacement therapy in postmenopausal women and cardiovascular disease: an overview. *Obstetrics and Gynaecology Survey*; 47: 426-431.
8   McPherson K. 1994. The best and the enemy of the good: randomised controlled trials, uncertainty, and assessing the role of patient choice in medical decision making. *Journal of Epidemiology and Community Health*; 48: 6-15.
9   Posthuma WFM, Westendorp RGJ, Vandenbroucke JP. 1994. Cardioprotective effect of hormone replacement therapy in postmenopausal women: is the evidence biased? *British Medical Journal*; 308: 1268-1269.
10 Bergkvist L, Adami H-O, Persson I, Bergstrom R, Krusemo UB. 1989. Prognosis after breast cancer diagnosis in women exposed to estrogen and estrogen-progestogen replacement therapy. *American Journal of Epidemiology*; 130: 221-228.
11 McMahon B, Cole P, Brown J. 1983. Etiology of human breast cancer: a review. *Journal of National Cancer Institute*; 50: 21-43.
12 Steinberg KK, Thacker SB, Smith SJ et al. 1991. A meta-analysis of the effect of estrogen replacement therapy on the risk of breast cancer. *Journal of the American Medical Association*; 265: 1985-1990.
13 Bergkvist L, Adami H-O, Persson I, Hoover R, Schairer C. 1989. The risk of breast cancer after estrogen and estrogen-progestin replacement. *New England Journal of Medicine*; 321: 293-297.

14 Barrett-Connor E. 1994. Postmenopausal estrogen and the risk of breast cancer. *Annals of Epidemiology*; 4: 177-180.

15 Daly E, Roche M, Barlow D, Gray A, McPherson K, Vessey M. 1992. HRT: An analysis of benefits, risks and costs. *British Medical Bulletin*; 48: 368-400.

16 Daly E, Vessey MP, Barlow D, Gray A, McPherson K, Roche M. 1993. *Proceedings of the 7th International Congress on the Menopause*. Stockholm.

17 Daly E, Gray A, Barlow D, McPherson K, Roche M, Vessey M. 1993. Measuring the impact of menopausal symptoms on quality of life. *British Medical Journal*; 307: 836-840.

18 Vines G. 1993. The challenge to HRT. *New Scientist*; 23/10/93: 21-23.

19 Wilkes H. 1994. Personal communication to Imogen Sharp.

20 McPherson K. 1991. Latent effects in the interpretation of any association between oral contraceptives and breast cancer. *The proceedings of the 4th International Symposium of Benign Breast Disease*. Parthenon.

21 Stevenson JC, Whitehead MI. 1990. Breast cancer and estrogen replacement. *New England Journal of Medicine;* 322: 201-202.

CHAPTER 10

Physical activity

Physical activity: how does it affect women's risk of CHD?

ADRIANNE E HARDMAN

SUMMARY
Research suggests that physical inactivity is an independent risk factor for coronary heart disease (CHD) among men, and that regular physical activity reduces the risk. There is growing evidence that even moderate physical activity is sufficient to confer a benefit. Although there is insufficient evidence to conclude that physical activity is an *independent* risk factor for women, there is evidence that it might modify some of the risk factors for CHD such as lipoprotein levels, high blood pressure, obesity and adult-onset diabetes.

Cross-sectional studies among women indicate that although exercise seems to have little effect on total cholesterol, it has a positive effect on HDL cholesterol among both endurance trained women and those taking more moderate amounts of exercise such as walking. Longitudinal studies provide some evidence that endurance training increases HDL cholesterol in women, but more longitudinal studies among women are needed. Changes in lipoprotein levels are more marked when the programme is accompanied by weight loss.

Given the low levels of physical activity among women in the UK, a large proportion of women may be at increased risk of CHD because of their inactivity.

Epidemiological evidence

Over 40 epidemiological studies, predominantly cohort studies, have examined the risk of coronary heart disease (CHD) in physically active men compared to their sedentary counterparts. Few, however, provide information about women.

Evidence among men

Some of the strongest evidence of an inverse relationship between physical activity and CHD in men comes from studies of Harvard University graduates. The influence of leisure time physical activity on the incidence of CHD was examined in cohorts of alumni who had entered the university between 1916 and 1950.[1] Long-term follow-up showed that the risk of first heart attack was 64% higher among men who used up less than 2,000 kilocalories per week in physical activity in middle age than in those with a higher activity index. Moreover, graduates who walked nine or more miles a week had a 21% lower risk of death from all causes than those who walked less than three miles a week.[2] Moderate amounts of physical activity thus appeared to be protective in these men.

Studies of executive grade civil servant office workers in the UK, however, found that only those men who reported taking part in 'vigorous' physical activity in their leisure time on initial survey in 1968-70 had a lower risk of CHD than sedentary men.[3,4] In this study the definition of 'vigorous' activity was exercise which has a peak energy expenditure of about 7.5 kilocalories per minute: the equivalent to walking at just over four miles an hour.

Debate about the amount and intensity of physical activity needed for protection against CHD is unresolved and differences between studies in the United States and the UK may, in part, be attributable to differences in the cohorts of men involved.

However, there is growing evidence that moderate physical activity may be sufficient to confer benefit. Firstly, nine-year follow-up of a separate group of 9,000 civil servants found that those men who reported that they often participated in vigorous sports and did considerable bouts of cycling, or those who reported that their regular speed of walking was more than four miles an hour, had an attack rate of non-fatal and fatal CHD which was less than half of that of the men who did not report such activity.[5] Secondly, results from the British Regional Heart Study indicate that the relationship between a low physical activity index and the risk of CHD was not weakened even when the data for those men who reported doing sporting (vigorous) activity at least once a month were excluded.[6]

Overall, the epidemiological studies in middle-aged men have found a median relative risk of physical inactivity of 1.9. No study has found a *higher* incidence of CHD in active men and, for the better studies the relative risk is increased to 2.4.[7] Powell and colleagues therefore appear justified in concluding that:

> *"The relative risk of physical inactivity is similar in magnitude to that associated with hypertension, hypercholesterolaemia and smoking."* [7]

Thus, 40 years of research carried out in many countries strongly support the suggestion that physical inactivity is an independent risk factor for CHD in men, and that regular physical activity reduces this risk.

Evidence among women

In contrast, there is insufficient evidence to conclude that physical inactivity is an independent risk factor for CHD in women. No individual study has addressed the question and few studies have presented data separately for women.

Of the seven known studies which included women, three found no association between physical activity and CHD risk,[8, 9, 10] three an inverse association,[11, 12, 13] and one an inverse association for angina but not for myocardial infarction or CHD death.[14] Thirty-year follow-up of women in the Framingham study showed that, among 50-59 year olds, women with CHD were less likely to have been physically active, but this effect disappeared after controlling for standard risk factors.[8]

As physical activity was not a central concern in any of these seven studies, however, the methods of describing such activity were not as comprehensive as those used in the studies of men, thus decreasing the likelihood of finding a relationship between physical activity level and CHD risk.[7]

Physical inactivity necessarily results in low levels of fitness. Evidence from a study of 3,120 women over an eight-year period shows that age-adjusted deaths from all causes (overwhelmingly cardiovascular disease) declined with increasing levels of physical fitness.[15] The relationship was strong, with a particularly high mortality rate among women in the lowest fitness quintile (who had a relative risk of 4.6 compared with the highest quintile) and consistent for women and men. Moreover, it held after adjustment for the major cardiovascular risk factors.

Thus there is insufficient evidence to conclude that physical inactivity is an *independent* risk factor for women. However, there is evidence that physical activity can modify some of the risk factors for CHD in women, such as lipoprotein levels, high blood pressure, obesity and adult-onset diabetes.

How physical activity affects lipoprotein metabolism

There is uncertainty concerning both the mechanism by which physical activity might lead to a reduction in CHD risk and the extent to which such benefit can be acquired through a programme of physical activity which large numbers of people are prepared to follow. Mechanisms suggested include an effect on the acute phase of CHD, for example by inhibiting clotting,[5] and an influence on lipoprotein metabolism.[16]

It has been known for some time that endurance-trained female athletes have more favourable lipoprotein profiles than sedentary women. Exercise seems to have little effect on total cholesterol concentration, but has a positive effect on HDL cholesterol which is beneficial. Endurance-trained women have higher plasma HDL cholesterol levels than sedentary controls[17] which cannot be attributed to differences in age, relative weight, total cholesterol or triglycerides.[18]

From a public health point of view, it is important to establish whether the more modest amounts of physical activity, which a lot of women might do, confer a noticeable benefit. Studies have shown that this is the case. The Lipid Research Clinic's Prevalence Study, for example, found higher levels of HDL cholesterol in physically active women: these differences were significant in 20-29 and 30-39 year olds.[19] Comparison of lipoprotein levels in women endurance runners, members of the local rambling club and sedentary controls suggests that there is a 'dose-response' relationship: both HDL cholesterol and HDL_2 cholesterol were higher in runners than in walkers, and higher in walkers than in controls.[20] These data are consistent with the studies which have shown that patients who are immobilised for long periods have low HDL cholesterol levels, while exercisers tend to have high levels. Thus the HDL benefit is also found in women who take more moderate amounts of exercise.

Evidence from the cross-sectional studies described above is beset by problems, since it might be that people with particular predispositions tend to take up exercise. Longitudinal studies are therefore important. Existing evidence from such studies provides only weak supportive evidence that endurance training increases HDL cholesterol in women. This may be partly because most have lasted only a relatively short period of time. To date there have been nine such longitudinal studies involving women: five uncontrolled and four controlled.

Of the five uncontrolled longitudinal studies of endurance training in women, one found an increase in HDL cholesterol,[21] two found no change in HDL cholesterol[22, 23] and one reported a significant increase in the HDL/LDL ratio in obese women.[24] Brownell and colleagues[25] found a small decrease in HDL cholesterol in women but an increase in men, and suggested that there might be a sex difference in the response of lipoprotein metabolism to exercise training.

One of the four controlled studies of exercise training, by Boyden and colleagues,[26] found no change in lipoprotein metabolism with an eight-month walk-jog programme in women with an average age of 51 years, despite evidence of improved endurance fitness. In another study involving older, post-menopausal women, just eight weeks of walking (70%-80% of predicted maximal heart rate for 40 minutes, three times a week) had the effect of increasing HDL cholesterol and decreasing both triglycerides and the ratio of total to HDL cholesterol. Body fat was also reduced.[27] The longest controlled study reported so far involved a flexible, unsupervised programme of brisk walking for one year.[28] At the end of the study, which resulted in improved endurance fitness,[29] HDL cholesterol was increased markedly for walkers relative to controls. In addition, the ratio of total to HDL cholesterol was decreased. Body fatness was not reduced. This study therefore indicates that, with a fairly modest programme of exercise, one can increase HDL cholesterol levels in women. This finding was confirmed in a controlled study in which regular slow, brisk and fast walking (over 24 weeks) were found to have similar effects on increasing HDL cholesterol levels.[30]

The evidence of a role for physical activity in modifying lipoprotein metabolism in women is therefore equivocal. Additional data are needed, ideally from randomised controlled trials, before any conclusions can be drawn.

Possible mechanisms by which physical activity might influence lipoprotein metabolism

The mechanism by which physical activity influences lipoprotein metabolism is still under debate, and may or may not be independent of a reduction in body fat. Changes in lipoprotein levels are more marked when the physical activity programme is accompanied by weight loss.[31] However, in some studies of endurance training in women, changes in lipoprotein levels were noted even where weight remained the same. These changes included a decrease in total cholesterol, triglyceride and LDL cholesterol, and an increase in HDL cholesterol.

Local changes in trained skeletal muscle probably also play a role.[32] One possibility is that training increases the activity of the enzyme lipoprotein lipase, by improving microcirculation in muscle. This enzyme hydrolyses the triglyceride of triglyceride-rich lipoproteins and during this process HDL_2 (the subfraction of HDL which is increased in active individuals and is inversely associated with CHD risk), is derived from HDL_3. Elegant experiments where only one leg is trained have shown that HDL_2 is produced from trained muscle during exercise but not from untrained muscle.[33]

Physical activity among women

Consistently, studies have shown that inactivity is widespread in women. The findings of Heartbeat Wales (now the Health Promotion Authority for Wales) suggest that, in the 35-65 age group, 73%-86% of women are 'minimally active or sedentary'.[34] Similarly, the Health and Lifestyle Survey[35] indicates that 50%-

70% of women aged between their late teens and early 40s do not take regular exercise, and among older women the proportion who are physically inactive is even higher. The 1990 National Fitness Survey found that, among women, 91% of 16-24 year olds and 93% of 25-34 year olds fell below the target level of physical activity needed to achieve a health benefit. Furthermore, women in manual social groups – who are at greatest risk of CHD – are least active.[36]

In order to have an impact on the risk of CHD, exercise has to use the body's large muscle groups. At least some of the benefit is probably conferred by an effect on muscles. The more muscle that is used in exercise, the better. Women often report that they are moving around a lot during the day, during the course of their housework or paid work. However, the sort of activity done during a day's work is often not sufficiently sustained to confer a CHD benefit.

Women are less likely to participate in vigorous activity, mainly for social and cultural reasons. A given exercise task is often relatively harder for women than for men. This is because a woman typically has a lower functional capacity. Consequently, the oxygen requirement of the exercise – similar for women and men – usually represents a higher proportion of functional capacity (maximal oxygen uptake) for women. When women and men exercise at a common intensity relative to their own maximal oxygen uptake, however, the level of cardiovascular and hormonal responses are very similar.

However, activity does not necessarily have to be sporting – or involve expensive equipment or fashionable clothing – in order to be beneficial. The potential to use the body as a means of transport, in walking or cycling, for example, needs to be emphasised in any public education. An individual could expend a larger amount of energy for example just by walking one mile to work or to the shops each day, than by going to an aerobics class once a week.

Conclusion

Although there is not enough epidemiological evidence to draw a conclusion about a direct relationship between physical activity and the risk of CHD for women, it seems reasonable to conclude that at least some aspects of the risk factors for CHD – such as lipoprotein levels, high blood pressure, obesity and adult-onset diabetes – might be modified by physical activity. It is biologically plausible that women may gain benefits similar to those which have been demonstrated in men.

Given the low prevalence of physical activity among women, a large proportion of women may be at increased risk of CHD because of their inactivity.

From the public health point of view, evidence that socially acceptable and attainable amounts of physical activity are effective in reducing the risk of CHD is encouraging.

This section is based on a paper prepared for the National Forum for Coronary Heart Disease Prevention by Dr Adrianne E Hardman, Senior Lecturer in the Department of Physical Education, Sports Science and Recreation Management, Loughborough University.

References

1 Paffenbarger RS, Wing AL, Hyde RT. 1978. Physical activity as an index of heart attack risk in college alumni. *American Journal of Epidemiology*; 108: 161-75.

2 Paffenbarger RS, Hyde RT, Wing AL, Hsieh C. 1986. Physical activity, all-cause mortality and longevity of college alumni. *New England Journal of Medicine*; 314: 605-613.

3 Morris JN, Chane SPW, Adam C, Sirey C, Epstein L, Sheehan DJ. 1973. Vigorous exercise in leisure-time and the incidence of coronary heart disease. *Lancet*; i: 333-339.

4 Morris JN, Everitt MG, Pollard R, Chave SPW. 1980. Vigorous exercise in leisure-time. Protection against coronary heart disease. *Lancet*; ii: 1207-1210.

5 Morris JN, Clayton DG, Everitt MG, Semmence AM, Burgess EH. 1990. Exercise in leisure time: coronary attack and death rates. *British Heart Journal*; 63: 325-334.

6 Shaper AG, Wannamethee G. 1991. Physical activity and ischaemic heart disease in middle-aged British men. *British Heart Journal*; 66: 384-394.

7 Powell KE, Thompson PD, Casperson CJ, Kendrick JS. 1987. Physical activity and the incidence of coronary heart disease. *Annual Review of Public Health*; No. 8: 253-287.

8 Eaker ED, Castelli WP. 1987. Coronary heart disease and its risk factors among women in the Framingham study. In *Coronary heart disease in women*: 122-30. (Eds Eaker ED, Packard B, Wenger NK, Clarkson TB, Tyroler HA.) New York: Haymarket Doyma.

9 Lapidus L, Bengtsson C. 1986. Socio economic factors and physical activity in relation to cardiovascular disease and death: a 12 year follow up of participants in a population study of women in Gothenberg, Sweden. *British Heart Journal*; 55: 295-301.

10 Bush TL, Criqui MH, Cowan LD, Barrett-Connor E, Wallace RB, Tyroler HA, Suchindran CM, Cohn R, Rifkind BM. 1987. Cardiovascular disease mortality in women: results for the Lipid Research Clinics follow-up study. In *Coronary heart disease in women*: 106-111. (Eds Eaker ED, Packard B, Wenger NK, Clarkson TB, Tyroler HA.) New York: Haymarket Doyma.

11 Magnus K, Matroos, Strackee J. 1979. Walking, cycling or gardening, with or without seasonal interruption, in relation to acute coronary events. *American Journal of Epidemiology*; 110: 724-733.

12 Salonen JT, Puska P, Tuomilehto J. 1982. Physical activity and risk of myocardial infarction, cerebral stroke and death. A longitudinal study in eastern Finland. *American Journal of Epidemiology*; 115: 526-537.

13 Wingard DL, Cohn BA. 1987. Coronary heart disease mortality among women in Alameda County, 1965-73 in *Coronary heart disease in women*: 99-105. (Eds Eaker ED, Packard B, Wenger NK, Clarkson TB, Tyroler HA.) New York: Haymarket Doyma.

14 Brunner D, Manelis G, Modan M, Levin S. 1974. Physical activity at work and the incidence of myocardial infarction, angina pectoris and death due to ischemic heart disease: an epidemiological study in Israeli collective settlements (kibbutzim). *Journal of Chronic Diseases*; 27: 217-233.

15 Blair SN, Kohl HW, Paffenbarger RS, Clark DG, Cooper KH, Gibbons LW. 1989. Physical fitness and all-cause mortality. A prospective study of healthy men and women. *Journal of the American Medical Association*; 262: 2395-2401.

16 Haskell WL. 1986. The influence of exercise training on plasma lipids and lipoproteins in health and disease. In *Physical activity in health and disease.* (Eds Astrand P-O, Grimby G.) *Acta Medica Scandinavica*; Suppl. 711: 25-37.

17 Moore CE, Hartung GH, Mitchell RE, Kappus CM, Hinderlitter J. 1983. The relationship of exercise and diet on high-density lipoprotein cholesterol levels in women. *Metabolism*; 32: 189-196.

18 Nakamura N, Uzawa H, Haeda H, Inomoto T. 1983. Physical fitness: its contribution to serum high density lipoprotein. *Atherosclerosis*; 48: 173-183.

19 Haskell WL, Taylor HL, Wood PD, Schrott H, Heiss G. 1980. Strenuous physical activity, treadmill exercise test performance and plasma high-density lipoprotein cholesterol. *Circulation*; 62 (suppl IV): 53-61.

20 Hardman AE, Hudson A, Hollington A. 1991. Plasma lipoprotein parameters in women endurance runners, walkers and controls. *Journal of Sports Science*; 9: 417.

21 Farrell PA, Barboriak J. 1980. The time course of alterations in plasma lipid and lipoprotein concentrations during eight weeks of endurance training. *Atherosclerosis*; 37: 231-238.

22 Frey MA, Doerr BM, Lauback LL, Mann BL, Glueck CJ. 1982. Exercise does not change high-density lipoprotein cholesterol in women after ten weeks of training. *Metabolism*; 31: 1142-1146.

23 Lipson LC, Bonow RO, Schaefer EJ, Brewer HB, Lindgren FT. 1980. Effect of exercise conditioning on plasma high density lipoproteins and other lipoproteins. *Atherosclerosis*; 37: 529-538.

24 Lewis S, Haskell WL, Wood PD, Manoogian N, Bailey JE, Pereira MB. 1976. Effects of physical activity on weight reduction in obese middle-aged women. *American Journal of Clinical Nutrition*; 29: 151-156.

25 Brownell KD, Barboriak PS, Ayerle RS. 1982. Changes in plasma lipid and lipoprotein levels in men and women after a program of moderate exercise. *Circulation*; 65: 477-484.

26 Boyden TW, Pamenter RW, Rotkis TC, Morrison DA, Freund BJ, Stanforth PR, Wilmore JH. 1987. Effects of exercise training on plasma high-density lipoprotein cholesterol, and sex steroid concentrations in women. In *Coronary heart disease in women*: 158-163. (Eds Eaker ED, Packard B, Wenger NK, Clarkson TB, Tyroler HA.) New York: Haymarket Doyma.

27 Whitehurst M, Menendex E. 1991. Endurance training in older women. Lipid and lipoprotein responses. *Physician and Sports Medicine*; 19: 95-103.

28 Hardman AE, Hudson A, Jones PRM, Norgan NG. 1989. Brisk walking and plasma high density lipoprotein cholesterol concentration in previously sedentary women. *British Medical Journal*; 299: 1204-1205.

29 Hardman AE, Jones PRM, Norgan NG, Hudson A. 1992. Brisk walking improves endurance fitness without changing body fatness in previously sedentary women. *European Journal of Applied Physiology and Occupational Physiology*; 65(4): 354-359.

30 Duncan JJ, Gordon NF, Scott CB. 1991. Women walking for health and fitness. How much is enough? *Journal of the American Medical Association*; 266: 3295-3299.

31 Tran ZV, Weltman A. 1985. Differential effects of exercise on serum lipid and lipoprotein levels seen with changes in body weight: a meta-analysis. *Journal of the American Medical Association*; 254: 919-924.

32 Thompson PD. 1990. What do muscles have to do with lipoproteins? *Circulation*; 81: 1428-1430.

33 Kiens B, Lithell H. 1989. Lipoprotein metabolism influenced by training-induced changes in human skeletal muscle. *Journal of Clinical Investigation*; 83: 558-564.
34 Welsh Heart Programme Directorate. 1987. *Exercise for health in Wales. Findings from the Welsh Heart Health Survey. Heartbeat report No. 23.* Cardiff: Heartbeat Wales.
35 Blaxter M. 1987. *The health and lifestyle survey.* The Health Promotion Research Trust.
36 Activity and Health Research. 1992. *Allied Dunbar national fitness survey: a report on activity patterns and fitness levels: Commissioned by the Sports Council and the Health Education Authority.* London: Sports Council and Health Education Authority.

Patterns of physical activity among women: what are the policy implications?

DUSTY RHODES

SUMMARY

Eight out of ten women fall below the level of physical activity needed to achieve a health benefit. Despite the increase in popularity of aerobics, swimming and keep fit during the 1980s, only a minority of women participate in any form of regular physical activity. Physical activity levels are particularly low among older women and women from lower socioeconomic groups.

Several factors influence women's physical activity levels. Firstly, attitudes held both by women and by society. Women may not value participation for themselves, may perceive themselves as fitter than they are, and may be influenced by negative experiences of physical education at school. Secondly, domestic responsibilities and lack of time are further barriers to participation. Thirdly, many exercise and sports facilities are uninviting for women. Fear of traffic and lack of street lighting may also deter women from activities such as walking and cycling.

Campaigns to increase women's activity levels should avoid the term 'sport', which many women find off-putting, and focus on fitting physical activity into daily life. They must take into account women's main reasons for taking exercise: to lose weight or to look good. Physical activity needs to be presented as a positive experience: schools need to provide a range of activities for girls. Women who take regular exercise when young are more likely to continue in later life.

Local alliances of health authorities, local authorities, adult education and sports development agencies can help to increase opportunities for physical activity among women. Campaigns need to focus on maintaining as well as triggering change.

There has been growing concern about the low numbers of women involved in sport and recreation since the mid-1970s. Many public sector providers attempted to address the problem by developing policies and strategies to encourage women to take up some form of physical activity. Much of this work was carried out in the mid-80s and early 90s. Of the recent national policies relevant to the issue of women, the most significant is probably the Sports Council's 'Sport for All' initiative, established in the mid-80s.

It is difficult to determine the precise effect of such initiatives because of a lack of monitoring by key agencies. Policy has not been based on reliable information on, for example, patterns and frequency of participation, and motivational factors.

Until recently, there has been little reliable data on women's involvement in physical activity and sport in the UK, and an almost complete lack of research in regard to women's participation at all levels. Although the General Household Survey[1] provides information on general trends in participation in physical activity, it does not give information about participation levels in specific groups such as working class women, single parents, women with disabilities, or women from ethnic minority groups. Nor does it assess frequency or patterns of physical activity, or the motivating factors which encourage women to participate in sport or recreation or other related physical activities.

The National Fitness Survey,[2] which assessed the activity and fitness levels in 6,000 English adults in 1990, begins to address some of these issues.

The Health of the Nation Physical Activity Task Force, established in 1993, could play a crucial role in addressing women's needs in this area.

Participation

According to data from the General Household Survey, only a minority of women who have left school participate in any form of regular physical activity. Participation rates decline with age, and the lowest participation rates are among women over the age of 60.

During the period 1983-88, women were a target group for activities by the Sports Council and by some local authority leisure and recreation departments. Figures 1 and 2 show changes in the numbers and percentages of women participating in indoor and outdoor sport during this period. Participation by women in indoor activities increased from 19.5% in 1983 to 24.2% in 1988 (see Figure 1). The increase was found in all age groups, but was greatest among younger women. During the same period, however, women's participation in outdoor activities fell very slightly from 25% to 24.3%, and the decrease was greater among younger women (see Figure 2). Overall, health-related activities, including swimming, fitness training, aerobics and jogging, increased among the over-30s. Participation rates were lowest for women over 60 years, but the campaign aimed at the over-50s improved participation during this five-year period.

FIGURE 1: Changes in the percentage of women, by age, participating in indoor sport, 1983-88

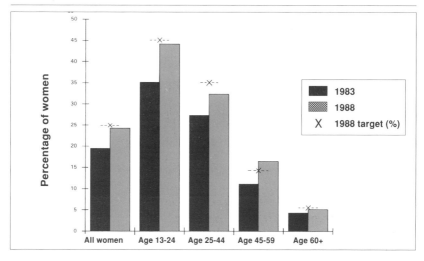

Source: See reference 3.

FIGURE 2: Changes in the percentage of women, by age, participating in outdoor sport, 1983-88

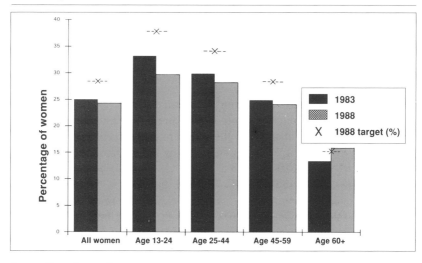

Source: See reference 3.

Despite these changes in participation, the National Fitness Survey[2] found that in 1990 over eight out of ten women fell below the level of physical activity needed to achieve a health benefit. Even among 16-24 year old women, the figure was 91%. The survey also found that nearly two-thirds of women would find it difficult to sustain walking at a reasonable pace (3 mph) up a 1 in 20 slope. The proportion rises from 34% among 16-24 year old women, to 92% among 65-74 year old women. Even walking on ground level at 3 mph is severe exertion for many older women: over half (55%) of older women are not fit enough to continue walking on the level at this speed.

The social class differences among women are also marked. In the National Fitness Survey, 21% of women in the semi-skilled and unskilled classes (IV and V) were in activity level 0 (no activity of moderate or vigorous intensity lasting for at least 20 minutes in the previous four weeks), compared to 13% in professional and intermediate groups (classes I and II).

The survey found that swimming, exercises and social dancing are the three most popular sport and active recreation activities: but the only activities in which the participation of women exceeded that of men were social dancing, keep fit, and aerobics.

Factors influencing participation

When planning any campaign aimed at increasing women's participation, it is important to understand why women place such a low value on physical activity, and to take into account the factors influencing participation. These include: attitudes; time, money and domestic responsibilities; role models; and facilities.

Attitudes
The single most difficult barrier to overcome is attitudes. Sport and exercise in the UK are regarded by many as a predominantly male activity. This is borne out by greater participation rates among men than women.

A large study in Sheffield in 1987,[4] involving interviews with 2,000 women, found that women did not relate to the words 'sport and recreation'. The terms were seen as male words, and conjured up images of competitiveness, aggression and activities that had little meaning in women's lives. In the National Fitness Survey, the perception that they were 'not the sporty type' was a deterrent for 38% of women; this perception was even greater among older women.[2]

Society holds many double standards in terms of which types of physical activity are acceptable for women. For example, it is perfectly acceptable for women to participate in a local aerobics class, but perhaps less acceptable for young women to play rugby or to take up other active sports which are more traditionally male. These social attitudes are problematic as they are fundamental to the whole question of women's participation.

Women's own attitudes may be influenced by negative experiences of physical education at school, even at primary school. The development of a negative attitude from a young age will have a very strong influence on the way women regard physical activity when they are older. Activity declines markedly with increasing age, and people who exercise regularly in their youth are more likely to continue or to resume exercise in later years.[2]

Furthermore, women do not necessarily see the value of participation for themselves. As in other areas of their lives, women often do not value their own needs, and put the needs of others, such as children and the family, first. For a variety of reasons, many women do not make their own leisure or health care a priority, and do not therefore invest in a long-term commitment to regular physical activity.

They may also perceive themselves to be fitter and more active than they actually are. For example, in the National Fitness Survey, 57% of women in activity level 0 believed themselves to be very or fairly active.[2]

Racist attitudes and cultural factors may make it more difficult for women from black and ethnic minority communities to participate in physical activity. This may be particularly important for Asian women, who have high rates of CHD and for whom physical activity may be especially important.

Disabled women face different barriers: the stereotypes of disability make it difficult for disabled women to participate in exercise in a regular and integrated way. Health professionals and those working in local authority leisure and recreation services may be well placed to help address some of these issues.

Of all the factors influencing women's participation, attitudes may be the most difficult to challenge and change. To address this problem, a long-term education programme is needed, with the support of key agencies such as schools, youth clubs, the media, employers, local authorities, sports and recreation agencies, and health promotion agencies. The issue could be tackled on a national level by the Health of the Nation Physical Activity Task Force.

Time, money and domestic responsibilities

Time is often a major problem, particularly for women who are employed and have domestic responsibilities. The Sheffield study[4] found that lack of time was the single most important factor influencing participation. The issue is not only limited time, but also when that time is: for example, it may not be until late at night when tiredness, lack of facilities or lack of a safe environment acts as a constraint.

Organising the family, or finding time when both partners can leave the children, is another constraint. Many women find it difficult to make time for themselves within the family. The National Fitness Survey found that domestic responsibilities – including marriage, childcare, and setting up home – were among the main barriers to taking part in sport and recreation, particularly for mothers of young children.[2] There is a need to promote more activities which can be done with the family. Walking, cycling and swimming are examples, but do require either daylight, or organisation and time.

Other factors, such as lack of money, are related to social class, and there is a social class gradient in participation. Women in social classes I and II are more likely to participate than women in social classes IV and V. When there is very little money, leisure activities are not a priority. It is often difficult for women to sustain a programme of exercise and sport, as their circumstances may change frequently.

The focus should be on fitting in physical activity with everyday activities, such as walking the mile to work or the shops, and on identifying part of the day when women could do some activity on their own.

Role models

There is a serious lack of role models promoting the positive aspects of physical activity for women. There are very few well known sportswomen for women and girls to recognise and identify with. The media has a major role to play in promoting positive female role models, in sport and active living. Yet studies show that, on average, only 3% of the total sports coverage is women's sport in both the national and tabloid press.[5]

Facilities

Facilities for exercise are often uninviting for women. Facilities include the provision of a safe environment for activities such as walking and cycling. The fear of traffic and lack of street lighting can be a major disincentive for women.

The image projected by sports centres is often not very women-friendly, and the major programme of activities is often aimed at men. Private clubs and voluntary sporting organisations form the most common type of venue for sport in the UK.

Women often do not have the income to pay for exercise facilities. Also the formal set-up that these facilities offer is not particularly encouraging for women, especially for new participants or for women who have not taken part in any physical activity since school.

Exercise facilities also present additional barriers such as a lack of childcare, transport, and provision of only a narrow range of activities: women's use of facilities depends on the kinds of activities on offer. Many women have caring responsibilities for the family, and have less time for leisure than their partners or husbands. Consultation with women to ascertain their needs could improve accessibility, but it is often neglected.

Physical activity is also an important part of CHD rehabilitation programmes. However, many of these programmes offer facilities which cater more for men than women, and the drop-out rate among women is higher than among men (see Chapter 4). As physical activity can help in the rehabilitation process, it is important to ensure that rehabilitation programmes are more tailored to women's needs.

Policy implications

Legislative changes in the late 1980s, such as the introduction of compulsory competitive tendering and the Education Reform Act, have had a negative impact on participation by girls and women in physical activity. The carefully planned programmes of the 70s and 80s, aimed at encouraging women to adopt a more active lifestyle, are now in decline.

For example, the Local Government Act (1988) is having a profound effect on the type of services offered in the public sector. Compulsory competitive tendering is forcing local authorities to make leisure, sports and recreation facilities a profit-led service which may effectively exclude many women and girls, as the pricing will be beyond their means. Development work in the community, the most successful strategy to encourage the non-participant into physical activity programmes, is being cut and will be gradually eroded in most local authorities.

Future campaigns need to address the following important areas.

Planning national and local programmes to increase physical activity

Research, rather than guesswork, should inform the development and implementation of effective programmes and policies for women. It is important to define the aims of any education programme, whether short-term or long-term, and base them on existing information. At a national level, the Health of the Nation Physical Activity Task Force might help achieve this. At local level, alliances involving health authorities, local authorities, schools and the media, could be established to tackle this.

The emphasis needs to be on facilitating mass participation, and encouraging physical activity as part of daily life. The message that moderate as well as vigorous activity may have cardiovascular benefit needs to be conveyed to the public. The focus should be on ordinary activities that people can do regularly.

The term 'physical activity' needs to be used in preference to 'sport' and 'exercise', to help convey the message that people do not have to take part in sport in order to be physically active. The word 'sport' suggests an elitist and male activity, and is likely to be off-putting for many women. (It has been suggested that the Sports Council might consider changing its name, to emphasise physical activity rather than sport.)

Women and men differ in their stated reasons for taking exercise, and this needs to be taken into account in any policy or education strategy. Women are more likely to say they take exercise to lose weight or to look good; men are more likely to say that they take exercise because it is better for health, to feel fitter, or to have fun or relax.

Physical activity for girls and women needs to be presented as a very positive experience, from the beginning of schooling, and throughout life. Schools could help improve girls' participation in physical activity by widening the range of activities available and helping to create safe environments so that children can walk or cycle to school. The emphasis needs to be on encouraging participation in activities which girls will continue once they have left school.

It is important to stress the short-term as well as long-term benefits of regular physical activity: for example, that it can improve an individual's sense of well-being and have beneficial effects on self-concept, depression and possibly anxiety. Health education resources should emphasise that stress control and relaxation go hand in hand with good exercise.

Partnerships

Partnerships, or alliances, are crucial particularly when resources are scarce. Partnerships are very effective at bringing together people with different experiences who can together have an impact. They also help to avoid the duplication of resources, a common practice in the UK. At a local level, local authorities, health authorities, health promotion units, education authorities, and adult education and sports development agencies should be involved. Such local health and fitness campaigns have been particularly effective in attracting the over-30 age group.

Staffing and training

Before embarking on any campaign, it is important to take account of staff available and their skills. Key staff need expertise in recreation, community development and promotional techniques.

Training is important for both paid and unpaid staff, to ensure that people working on any programmes or campaigns are properly informed about the issues. If it is not possible to offer training sessions, training materials will need to be produced and provided for staff.

Promotional materials and techniques

Women need to identify with the images used to promote any programme or campaign. For example, women will not relate to a 'Sport for All' programme whose promotional material features only male sports personalities.

Campaigns should examine the promotional techniques which use women effectively and draw on this experience. Media interest is very important. The 'Friends for Fitness' project, carried out in conjunction with Thames Television, is a good example of the use of the media. The underlying message of the project for women was 'Find a friend and get fit'. It emphasised the social aspect of exercise, and was not dependent on facilities. Thames Television received some 7,000 positive responses to the initiative and, eight months later, over 50% of the women were still doing some form of activity. By finding a new way of addressing the issue of women's participation in physical activity, the project had enormous success.

Many health education campaigns focus on triggering rather than maintaining change. Every year, women attempt to change their diet, give up smoking, or take up regular physical activity. But the attempts often fail. There is a need for research to examine what is needed to make it easier for women to maintain the positive health changes that they have made.

Resources
The resources available clearly determine the type of programme, and money is usually a problem for sport and physical activity facilities. However, it becomes easier to reallocate resources if attitudes towards improving women's participation are positive. A long-term commitment to providing resources is needed, in order to sustain local physical activity programmes. Secure funding is needed: resources are often invested in starting up new programmes, but it is important that they are maintained if they are to have a lasting effect.

Conclusion

Physical activity has an important role to play in improving health and in preventing CHD.

Exercises, keep fit, swimming and dancing have been major growth areas over the past decade, but women are still minority participants in most indoor and outdoor sports and active recreation. One of the most significant findings of the National Fitness Survey was the very low proportion of women who reached higher levels of physical activity.

Women's low rates of participation need urgent attention, and represent a great challenge, not only to women themselves, but also for the organisations concerned with promoting their health and improving the quality of their lives through active living and sport.

Physical activity may also have many secondary benefits for women. For example, regular physical activity may cause women to re-assess other aspects of their lifestyle such as diet and smoking habits. The effect of exercise in improving self-concept and self-esteem could be an important issue in tackling smoking in young women. Further research should investigate these interrelationships.

Physical activity needs to be promoted as part of daily life, and the emphasis of any strategy needs to be on facilitating and encouraging mass participation on a regular basis, especially among girls and women. Improving the general physical and social environment is essential in promoting physical activity. For example, transport policy could, but often does not, encourage walking and cycling. If a safe environment is lacking, so too will be the motivation. The fear of traffic and the lack of street lighting can be a major disincentive.

The social constraints on participation need to be addressed by policy makers and planners at all levels.

This section is based on a paper prepared for the National Forum for Coronary Heart Disease Prevention by Dusty Rhodes, formerly Women's National Development Officer at the Women's Sports Foundation.

References

1   Office of Population Censuses and Surveys. *General household surveys.* London: HMSO.
2   Activity and Health Research. 1992. *Allied Dunbar national fitness survey: a report on activity patterns and fitness levels: Commissioned by the Sports Council and the Health Education Authority.* London: Sports Council and Health Education Authority.
3   Sports Council. 1988. *Into the nineties: A strategy for sport 1988-1993.* London: Sports Council.
4   Green E, Hebron S, Woodward D. 1987. *Gender and leisure: a study of Sheffield women's leisure.* London: Sports Council.
5   Women's Sports Foundation. 1992. *A survey of women's sports coverage in the media.* London: Women's Sports Foundation.

CHAPTER 11

Ideas for action

Chapter 3 sets out the Forum's major recommendations to address the high rates of coronary heart disease (CHD) among women in the UK. This chapter gives specific ideas for action that could be undertaken at various levels: by the European Union, through national policy, and by health authorities, local authorities, professional and academic bodies,workplaces, schools and youth clubs, the media and the voluntary sector.

Many prevention policies aimed at the general population are likely to be effective for both women and men. But while it is important to recognise the common issues which need to be tackled within a population strategy for CHD prevention, it is also important to recognise women's special needs.

Recognising women's risk of CHD is only the first step. Reducing this risk will involve many different policy measures, and a broad range of agencies. This chapter outlines the broad contribution of different sectors. The charts on pages 178-181 set out specific ideas for action to address women's needs, including fiscal and regulatory measures, education, service provision and research.

Coronary heart disease has traditionally been perceived as a man's disease. This report turns the spotlight on women and highlights their special needs in heart health. The concerns now need to be addressed.

European Union policy

Much policy affecting the health of the UK population, including women, is formulated at an international, and particularly European Union (EU), level.

Article 129 in the Maastricht Treaty, on public health, establishes a clear mandate for European Union action on public health. Cardiovascular diseases, including CHD and stroke, are a major cause of death and ill health across Europe. The European Commission's programme on public health could be used to formulate European policy and programmes which benefit women's heart health.

National policy

Policy makers, health professionals and individual women themselves, may not be sufficiently aware of women's risks as potential victims of CHD. It is important that this risk is addressed – both in terms of prevention and in the identification of possible symptoms of CHD. Women have been comparatively neglected in national CHD prevention campaigns and there is a need for a national campaign to increase awareness of their risk of CHD.

There is also a severe dearth of – and a real need for – research on women and CHD, to inform policy. Women have been excluded from many research studies, including studies on epidemiology, prevention, diagnosis, treatment and rehabilitation, and many areas of policy rely solely on extrapolation from male data. Research on CHD in women should be a priority, in order to inform national policy. More research is also needed on health-related behaviour and women's motivations for change, and on the risks and benefits of intervention in women.

Among women – as among men – there are social class, regional and ethnic differences in CHD. National policy also needs to address these inequalities, and the social and economic factors which affect the risk of CHD. This might include policies which address poverty among women, general education, childcare provision, and access to facilities. Women's motivations and the barriers to change also need to be addressed. Poor women, who have the highest rates of CHD, should be a focus of national policy.

It is important that health promotion strategies directed at women help lead to change, through policies which make healthy choices the easy choices, rather than simply providing information. Women often have much guilt and anxiety in relation to health issues such as eating and diet, smoking, and exercise: health education may simply reinforce that guilt.

National Health Service

The National Health Service has an important role not only in the direct education of patients and provision of services appropriate for women, but also as advocate on issues that affect women's risk of CHD, and in providing powerful examples to staff and to other employers. It is the UK's largest employer and women comprise 75% of its workforce.

In primary care, including well-person clinics, advice on reducing coronary risk needs to be offered to women as well as men: the potential for prevention of CHD among women is greater than for breast or cervical cancer. However, it is important that the advice given is appropriate for women, and that health professionals receive training and guidance in this area. The medical and nursing professions need information about interpreting CHD risk factors in women: interpretation of and advice on CHD risk factors must take sex and age into account.

Health professionals also need to recognise women's risk of CHD in order to help ensure that possible symptoms of CHD are identified, and appropriately followed up and treated.

Audit in the NHS could also include the investigation of sex differences in the various stages of CHD referral, including risk assessment, investigation, treatment and rehabilitation (patient to GP, to cardiologist, to surgeon).

Directors of Public Health need to use the contracting process to ensure that health service contracts include specific preventive measures, such as no-smoking policies, and advice to women on CHD risk reduction.

Directors of Public Health also have an important role in monitoring the work of all local agencies that impinge on heart health, in their annual public health report.

Local authorities

Women's low levels of physical activity need to be addressed locally as well as nationally. There is a need for local initiatives, particularly in inner city and rural areas, and for more leisure and recreation facilities which take women's special needs into account. If physical activity is to be promoted as part of women's daily lives, the social constraints will also need to be addressed by policy makers and planners. Women may be reluctant to walk by themselves at night, for example if street lighting is poor. Transport policy and town planning need to help create a safe environment.

Local authorities also have an important role in enforcing the law on sales of cigarettes to under-16 year olds: many under-age smokers will be girls.

Professional and academic bodies

Professional and academic bodies have an important role in providing education, training and guidelines for health professionals on CHD risk, prevention, diagnosis and treatment in women. There is also a need for much research on CHD in women, to inform both policy and practice. Academic researchers could help fill the gap.

Professional bodies and academic researchers also need to lead the policy debates on issues that affect women's heart health, such as hormone replacement therapy.

Workplaces

The workplace is an ideal venue to introduce health policies and education, and to carry out cross-sectional and prospective research. Employers with a large proportion of female employees, including the NHS, could effectively address women's needs in CHD prevention, through provision of information and policies on, for example, smoking, nutrition and physical activity.

Schools and youth clubs

Coronary heart disease prevention should begin early, and schools can help ensure this. Schools can provide both health education and a health promoting environment. A particular issue for girls is preventing them from taking up smoking. Schools could consider targeting girls separately for smoking education and cessation advice. Primary prevention of obesity should also begin in childhood, with a focus on good nutrition, and physical activity that girls will continue once they have left school. This may be particularly important for Asian girls, and cultural issues will need to be addressed.

Media

The UK has a media directly aimed at women, namely women's magazines, which could have an important impact in raising women's awareness of their risk of CHD. However, research shows that although most women's magazine editors claim to be concerned about the health of their readers, the magazines still convey mixed health messages. For example, a single magazine issue may contain tobacco advertisements and smoking fashion models alongside articles on giving up smoking, or recipes high in saturated fat next to articles on diet and heart disease. A health policy needs to govern both editorial and advertising.

Voluntary sector

The voluntary sector has much to contribute by providing information and education on women's risk of CHD to both the public and to health professionals, providing female-led facilities and classes, and commissioning research on CHD in women, including research on health behaviour. Funding agencies could improve the information base on CHD in women by supporting such research.

Consumer groups, including women's organisations and agencies concerned with the elderly, have an important role in raising awareness of women's risk of CHD, and campaigning for improved health service provision for women with CHD.

The following pages give specific suggestions for action, policy intervention and research at European Union and national level and by the NHS, local authorities, professional/academic bodies, workplaces, schools and youth clubs, the media and the voluntary sector.

	EUROPEAN UNION POLICY	NATIONAL POLICY	NHS	LOCAL AUTHORITIES	PROFESSIONAL/ ACADEMIC BODIES	WORKPLACE	SCHOOLS AND YOUTH CLUBS	MEDIA	VOLUNTARY SECTOR
FISCAL	Funding for research and education on women and CHD	Regular increases in tobacco tax above inflation	Funding for local initiatives on food and health, targeted at low income women	Pricing policies to encourage women's use of exercise facilities		Incentives for exercise, eg subsidised facilities and classes for women	Incentives for healthy options in school meals and nutritious meals for all children who want them		Fund research on CHD in women
REGULATORY AND LEGAL	Use of Article 129 in Maastricht Treaty to develop policy and programmes which benefit women's heart health	New strategies to tackle smoking among low income women	Contracts for health care to include specific preventive measures and individual advice to women on CHD risk reduction	More effective enforcement of ban on tobacco sales to children under 16	Include sex differences in CHD in curriculum and accreditation for health professionals	NHS as large employer of women to act as educator, advocate and example on CHD prevention in women	School smoking policy, including education and restrictions	Women's magazines to have policy on not taking tobacco advertising	Ensure women included in research studies on CHD
	Ban on tobacco advertising and promotion	Development of strategies to prevent and tackle overweight and obesity in girls and women	No-smoking policies in health authority and trust premises, including restrictions on nurses' smoking	Provide exercise facilities which take account of women's needs	Guidelines on CHD risk assessment in women and men	No-smoking policies at workplaces	Healthy eating policy covering tuck shops, vending machines and school meals	Avoid tobacco sponsorship	
	Comprehensive European food and nutrition policy which takes health into account	Social policy to benefit women, eg maternity and childcare provision	Discussion of policy implications of HRT	Town planning to encourage exercise in women, eg street lighting			Use of PE time in curriculum to encourage physical activity among girls		

	EUROPEAN UNION POLICY	NATIONAL POLICY	NHS	LOCAL AUTHORITIES	PROFESSIONAL/ACADEMIC BODIES	WORKPLACE	SCHOOLS AND YOUTH CLUBS	MEDIA	VOLUNTARY SECTOR
EDUCATION	Support information exchange and training on sex differences in CHD	National education campaign to improve women's awareness of CHD risk	Education of primary care team on CHD risk and risk factors in women	Train leisure centre staff to encourage physical activity in women, including black and ethnic minority women	Education of health professionals about women's risks of CHD, and prevention, diagnosis and treatment	Information for female employees about CHD risk and symptoms	Encourage positive attitudes to exercise in girls, and address girls' motivations	Articles on CHD in women, in mass media, women's magazines and professional journals	Training videos for health professionals on women's risks of CHD, including screening, tests, treatment and rehabilitation
	Provide reviews of evidence on effectiveness of interventions in women	Information on CHD risk and risk reduction among Asian women and diabetic women	Information for women on risk of CHD, and benefits and risks of interventions including uncertainties	Provide information on safe walking and cycle routes for women	Reviews of evidence, and guidelines on use of HRT	Provide information on health risks of smoking	Use of female images in education materials on physical activity	Use of non-smoking female models on fashion pages; avoid images of women smoking	Information for women on risks and symptoms of CHD, by heart charities, and agencies for women and the elderly
		Use of confident female role models in health education on smoking and exercise	Information on health risks of smoking, and smoking and oral contraceptive use	Information for retailers on under-age smoking in girls			Target smoking education and cessation advice to girls separately	Media campaign to promote physical activity among women, with positive role models, and emphasis on social aspects of exercise	Advice for Asian women on high risk of CHD and possibilities for reduction

	EUROPEAN UNION POLICY	NATIONAL POLICY	NHS	LOCAL AUTHORITIES	PROFESSIONAL/ ACADEMIC BODIES	WORKPLACE	SCHOOLS AND YOUTH CLUBS	MEDIA	VOLUNTARY SECTOR
SERVICE PROVISION	Support targeted smoking prevention and cessation activities for women	Guidance to health authorities on CHD in women, and model contracts for purchasing CHD services	Health promotion in primary care - including well-women clinics - to use overall CHD risk assessment, taking age and sex into account	Provision of 'female friendly' exercise facilities, including childcare, female-led classes and activities to appeal to women	Training for health professionals on women's risk of CHD	Provision of smoking cessation courses for female employees, eg nurses	Range of activities in PE lessons, to encourage activities which girls will continue once they have left school, eg aerobics and dancing	Recipes in women's magazines to be consistent with health messages, and to have nutrition labelling	Smoking cessation courses and advice for women, in context of women's lives
		Guidelines for CHD risk assessment in women for primary care teams	Cardiac rehabilitation programmes tailored to women's needs	Support for local initiatives to improve diet of women on low income	Guidelines on cardiac rehabilitation programmes for women, to encourage participation	Physical activity incentives and programmes for women at work	Smoking cessation advice and courses for girls	Development of low fat recipes	Rehabilitation support for women with CHD, including exercise
		National campaign to increase women's physical activity: avoid term 'sport', use female role models, address negative attitudes	Smoking cessation courses in context of women's lives, linked to contraception and pregnancy (including for nurses)	Provision of community and adult education for women	Validation and development of diagnostic tests for CHD in women, and advice to health professionals	Incentives and provision for education for women	Integrated approach to health education, including confidence- and skills-building		

	EUROPEAN UNION POLICY	NATIONAL POLICY	NHS	LOCAL AUTHORITIES	PROFESSIONAL/ ACADEMIC BODIES	WORKPLACE	SCHOOLS AND YOUTH CLUBS	MEDIA	VOLUNTARY SECTOR
RESEARCH AND MONITORING	Monitor international trends in women's rates of CHD and risk factors	Fund research into CHD risk, prevention, diagnosis, treatment and rehabilitation in women	Research on provision and cost-effectiveness of CHD risk assessment and advice for women in primary care	Monitor use of exercise facilities by women, and barriers to use	Research on socioeconomic and domestic factors affecting smoking uptake, maintenance and cessation in women	Industry (workforce) to be involved in surveys on CHD prevention, including women	Research on why girls smoke and interventions to help them quit	Monitor messages to women on CHD and risk factors	Funding agencies to fund research into women and CHD including risk factors, prevention, diagnosis, treatment and rehabilitation
	Monitor international differences in CHD morbidity and treatment rates among women	Primary prevention trials of cholesterol reduction in women	Monitor referral rates of women for diagnostic tests and treatment for CHD	Monitor enforcement of law on sales of cigarettes to children under 16	Research on factors affecting women's food choice	Monitor impact of no-smoking policy on women's smoking rates	Research on girls' preferences and motivations for physical activity	Consumer surveys on women's awareness of CHD risk by women's magazines	Research on social class and ethnic differences in CHD risk among women
		Long-term prospective trial on effects of HRT on CHD risk	Monitor women's participation in rehabilitation programmes		Research on sex differences in clinical presentation and pathogenesis of CHD		Monitor nutritional content of school meals		Research on impact of physical activity on CHD risk in women
		Research on women's health behaviour, and links between lifestyle factors, eg smoking and weight control, exercise and smoking	Directors of Public Health to do audit of sex differences in referral rates for CHD		Research on women's participation in cardiac rehabilitation programmes				Research on greater CHD risk among diabetic women and among Asian women

*Factfile
British Heart Foundation
The heart research charity

14 FITZHARDINGE STREET LONDON W1H 4DH TELEPHONE 071-935 0185 FAX 071-486 1273

1/93

WOMEN AND THE PREVENTION OF CORONARY HEART DISEASE

Coronary heart disease is usually perceived as a man's disease. Yet it is also the single greatest cause of death in women, both above and below the age of 65.

Women with coronary disease are most likely to present with angina, which is as common a disorder in women as it is in men. Painless myocardial infarction is common, particularly in older women. Although women live longer than men, their extra years of life are often years of disability: preventable or correctable chronic heart failure of ischaemic origin is a major contributor. Furthermore, there is evidence that women with heart disease are diagnosed and treated less promptly and less well than men.

Prevention is therefore important in women, but the approaches to it are slightly different from those in men.

Risk factors
The major risk factors for coronary heart disease are the same for women as for men, but they operate at a different level. Smoking, hypertension and raised blood cholesterol predominate, but for any given level, constitute a much smaller risk.

1. Teenage girls are now more likely to smoke than boys, and fewer women smokers stop compared with men. Women should be encouraged not to smoke or to stop if they already do so. Many women are reluctant to stop smoking because of fear of weight gain, but smoking should be the first target. Women on the contraceptive pill who also smoke have an increased risk of heart disease.

2. Blood cholesterol levels among women increase with age. From about age 50, and after the menopause, women's average cholesterol levels are higher than in men. The majority of older women have levels above the recommended cut-off points for intervention in men. By age 55, over 75% of women have levels above 6.5 mmol/l and 31% of women have levels over 7.8 mmol/l.

   However, for any given cholesterol level, women have roughly one-third the risk of men of developing coronary heart disease in the next six years. Part of this difference in risk may be due to women's relatively low triglyceride and high HDL cholesterol levels.

Blood cholesterol levels therefore need to be assessed in relation to age and sex (see last paragraph), and the threshold for therapy should therefore be higher for women. Definitive guidelines on treatment of hypercholesterolaemia must await evidence of the benefits of reducing cholesterol levels among women.

3. After age 45, women's average blood pressure is higher than men's. Blood pressure should be measured at least once every five years, and more regularly among women using oral contraceptives.

4. Obesity is linked to long-term risk of coronary heart disease among women, and the number of women who are overweight and obese is increasing. Weight should be measured at least once every five years. Overweight women should be advised to reduce their fat consumption and increase fruit and vegetable intake, and to become more physically active.

5. Exercise has a beneficial effect on the risk factors for coronary heart disease, particularly on HDL cholesterol. Middle-aged women have particularly low levels of exercise, and recent research suggests that eight out of ten women fall below the target level of physical activity needed for health benefit.

6. Oestrogen therapy has been shown to reduce the risk of coronary heart disease in post-menopausal women by up to 50 per cent. However, oestrogen-progestogen preparations, which are now more widely prescribed, may have less benefit. At present, there is insufficient evidence to conclude whether the benefits of combined hormone replacement therapy for cardiovascular risk outweigh the risks of increased breast cancer.

Diagnosis
Coronary disease is often diagnosed relatively late in women and there are particular diagnostic problems. For example, exercise electrocardiogram tests are more often 'false positive', ie ST changes occur in women with normal hearts.

Screening for risk factors
The potential for prevention of coronary heart disease among women is far greater than for breast cancer or cervical cancer. Overall (combined) risk factor assessment is as essential in women as in men.

Because there is doubt about the importance of cholesterol as a risk factor for women, measuring cholesterol in the absence of other risk factors is not recommended.

Factfile is produced by the British Heart Foundation in association with the British Cardiac Society and is compiled with the advice of a wide spectrum of doctors, including general practitioners. It reflects a consensus of opinion.

List of participants

The following people attended the National Forum's expert meeting in 1991, from which this report has developed.

Dr Amanda Amos, Department of Public Health Sciences,University of Edinburgh
Dr Margaret Ashwell, British Nutrition Foundation
Dr David Ashton, The London Heart Clinic
Ms Teresa Bahu, Anticipatory Care Teams
Dr Ian McLean Baird, British Heart Foundation
Dr Beulah Bewley, Action on Smoking and Health (ASH)
Mr Hedley Brown, Society of Cardiothoracic Surgeons
Dr Eric J Brunner, Department of Epidemiology and Public Health, University College of London
Ms Gill Cawdron, National Forum for Coronary Heart Disease Prevention
Mr C Cockbill, Ministry of Agriculture, Fisheries and Food
Ms Rovena Cohen, Welsh Office
Mr Dermot Collins, The Sports Council
Dr M A Church, Health Education Board for Scotland
Dr Jane Cope, Medical Research Council
Ms Jane Dawson, British Medical Journal
Ms Pauline Dimmock, Society of Health Education and Health Promotion Specialists
Mr Andrew P Dougal, Northern Ireland Chest, Heart and Stroke Association
Ms Elizabeth Dowler, Centre for Human Nutrition, London School of Hygiene and Tropical Medicine
Dr Richard Emanuel, Chest, Heart and Stroke Association
Dr Alun Evans, Department of Epidemiology and Public Health, Queen's University of Belfast
Dr Imogen Evans, The Lancet
Dr Fleur Fisher, British Medical Association
Prof John Goodwin, National Forum for Coronary Heart Disease Prevention
Ms Shirley Goodwin, King's Fund Institute
Mr Phelim Green, Department of Health and Social Services, Northern Ireland
Dr Adrianne Hardman, Department of Physical Education and Sports Science, Loughborough University
Ms Lucy Harris, National Consumer Council

Ms Eirlys Hayes, Health Promotion Authority for Wales
Ms Cathy Hulme, National Forum for Coronary Heart Disease Prevention
Ms Carol Humphries, Safeway plc
Ms Paula Hunt, Community Nutrition Group, British Dietetic Association
Dr Bobbie Jacobson, East London and The City Health Authority
Prof Philip James, The Rowett Research Institute
Ms Judith John, National Forum for Coronary Heart Disease Prevention
Prof Peter R M Jones, Department of Human Sciences, Loughborough University
Prof Desmond Julian, British Heart Foundation
Prof Kay-Tee Khaw, Clinical Gerontology Unit, University of Cambridge
Ms Helen King, Health Education Authority
Prof Dame June Lloyd, British Paediatric Association
Prof Michael Marmot, Department of Epidemiology and Public Health, University College of London
Dr Alan Maryon-Davis, Royal Institute of Public Health and Hygiene
Ms Liz McGranahan, Association of Primary Care Facilitators
Dr Diana McInnes, Department of Health
Prof Klim McPherson, Health Promotion Sciences Unit, London School of Hygiene and Tropical Medicine
Dr Hugh C Miller, Royal College of Physicians of Edinburgh
Ms Keng Mo, National Forum for Coronary Heart Disease Prevention
Ms Barbara Morgan, Family Heart Association
Dr Lotte Newman, Royal College of General Practitioners
Ms Vicki Nix, Royal College of Nursing
Mr Michael O'Connor, Coronary Prevention Group
Dr Noel Olsen, National Forum for Coronary Heart Disease Prevention
Dr Celia Palmer, Coronary Artery Disease Research Association (CORDA)
Prof Peter Quilliam, British Medical Association
Lord Rea, National Forum for Coronary Heart Disease Prevention
Ms Jean Rowe, Health Visitors' Association
Ms Dusty Rhodes, The Women's Sports Foundation
Dr Jennifer Roberts, Department of Public Health and Policy, London School of Hygiene and Tropical Medicine
Sir Keith Ross Bt, Royal College of Surgeons
Dame Rosemary Rue, British Medical Association
Ms Maggie Sanderson, British Dietetic Association
Ms Vibeke Schelleman, British Heart Foundation
Ms Imogen Sharp, National Forum for Coronary Heart Disease Prevention
Prof A G Shaper, Department of Public Health and Primary Care, Royal Free Hospital School of Medicine
Mr David Shaw, Department of Health Studies, Buckinghamshire College of Higher Education
Prof Desmond Sheridan, Royal College of Physicians of London

Dr John C Stevenson, Wynn Institute for Metabolic Research
Ms Linda Stone, Royal Pharmaceutical Society of Great Britain
Prof Hugh Tunstall-Pedoe, Cardiovascular Epidemiology Unit, University of Dundee
Ms Sarah Veale, Trades Union Congress
Ms Mary Walker, Department of Public Health and Primary Health Care, Royal Free Hospital School of Medicine
Ms Rhiannon Walters, Faculty of Public Health Medicine
Ms Heather Waring, British Heart Foundation
Dr Peter Whincup, Department of Public Health and Primary Health Care, Royal Free Hospital School of Medicine
Prof David Wood, National Heart and Lung Institute
Dr John Yarnell, Faculty of Public Health Medicine
Ms Andrea Young, Health Education Authority